unprepared

unprepared

Bob Shephard

TQL
PRESS
Oklahoma City, Oklahoma

© Copyright 2009
Bob Shephard
ISBN: 978-0-9824906-2-4
Printed in the United States of America
Design: Lyn Rayn

Published by TQL Press
P.O. Box 721243
Oklahoma City, OK 73172

This book is dedicated to all the people I have pastored who faced impossible life events and found themselves unprepared, but chose to trust God! You inspired me and hopefully some of your stories will inspire others to choose God.

I want to thank my wife, Faith Ann, for her love and support throughout our spiritual journey. To all of my children (Sharri, Jeff, Shelli, and Tami), their spouses, and my grandchildren, thank you for your support. May you walk in faith and obedience knowing God has got your back covered when you choose Him.

Thank you,
Bob, Dad, & Paps

contents

foreword

Dr. Robert Shephard has been my great friend for nearly 25 years. I have watched him grow as a leader, persevere in the midst of difficult circumstances and smile while dealing with the challenges of church ministry. He is a brother beloved to me.

It is with great anticipation and joy that I write the foreword for his book. Without question, *Unprepared* meets tragic circumstances of life with power packed answers and with a dynamic focus on the promises of God.

In this book, Dr. Shephard is the consummate storyteller. Each chapter unfolds a new story about real people who encounter real problems and discover real faith when confronted with the unexpected. I am unaware of any other book that has been written on this subject. As Robert Shephard states, "no matter if the unpreparedness is physical, financial, mental, emotional, or spiritual your decision to trust and give unconditional love will help you face every circumstance in life."

I believe this book is a needed resource for every pastor, counselor or church leader to assist members, friends, and loved ones through life's most difficult moments.

—Stan Toler
Bestselling Author
Oklahoma City, OK

preface

In writing Unprepared I hope to convey hope and help for anyone facing unexpected, overwhelming situations or even expected extremely difficult life decisions. So whether it is a tragic loss, or an unexpected call to care that might find you unprepared, choosing to place your trust in God, to forgive, and to live out unconditional love will bring you through as witnessed through the people in this book. Their life accounts of being caught unprepared will speak to you. No matter if the unpreparedness is physical, financial, mental, emotional, or spiritual, your decision to trust and to give unconditional love will help you face another moment, hour or even a month. In reading the accounts about real people who have faced horrific moments where demands, even for the simplest of decisions were daunting, you will see it is possible to be totally unprepared yet live to face another day.

1

unprepared

From the very recesses of your being comes the overwhelming thought, "I can not do this." Every cell of your body is communicating clearly you are unprepared for what you must face next. No person or supposedly soothing clichés from care-givers or counselors can provide the strength or comfort you really need. The temptation to go into isolation or to become a Walter Mitty fanatic, trying to operate in an unreal world rather than face what is ahead or what has just happened, is overwhelming. It is easy to go down either road, be it Isolation Interstate or Fantasy Freeway. It is also easy to get on the Anger Toll-way and pay the toll with the Blame Pass. The Pity-Poor-Me Road is always available, but it's a very dangerous road.

In reading Unprepared you will meet real people, like you and me, who have faced unthinkable, seldom talked about life events. These events, often devastating, and usually tragic, turned their lives upside down and inside out. Their microcosm collided with a macrocosm that rocked their private community. Shock and awe are lacking as words to describe the unprepared people you are about to meet. They were often faced with multiple difficult choices. These are people who ultimately choose to stop being a volunteer for more even though they have been the victim. Their stories and responses will encourage you that there is hope even when you are caught unprepared. For most of the people this choosing to stop being the volunteers for more "self-inflicted" pain didn't happen overnight. It took some time to choose to trust and to let the open wound of being a victim scab over. The scar is permanent but only a reminder of the tragedy and the pain. It is also a reminder that with a trust choice in God and His Holy Words one will be able to go on with life, even reaching the place of looking forward to a new day.

> There is One who will dry your unseen tears in the darkness.

As I communicate these accounts I vividly and tearfully remember each person and the unbelievable tragedies they endured. These are real stories. They are life stories of being caught unprepared. Only fictitious first names will be used for every individual whose story comes alive again on these pages. My prayer is that what they lived through will help someone else who finds themselves unprepared. My deepest desire and purpose for attempting to tell these real accounts is to help anyone who finds themselves unprepared.

My conclusion is we are all unprepared no matter how much we may believe otherwise. Take heart in your unpreparedness, there is One who will come alongside and even carry you if you need to be carried. There is One who will dry your unseen tears in the darkness, hold your hand on your lonely walk, and instill some new thoughts and comfort into your heart. Yes, He will even energize you with enough energy for your next moment, meeting or mind mandate. The people in the following chapters lived to face another day . . . Some of their stories seem unbelievable to me, yet I was there as their pastor, or friend, or family member, and Christian brother. They are my heroes, my encouragers, as I find myself unprepared to write, to tell their stories. Hopefully this attempt to communicate how they dealt with being unprepared will resonate to help others.

As Dr. Rueben Welch wrote years ago "we really do need each other." We need to know whom we can trust and Who will bring peace, healing and hope. We need to know we have a true Friend who helps us in our unpreparedness…as lived out in Chapter 2 by Connie in her loss of her family on Christmas Eve morning.

chapter 1

1. Have you ever faced something that made you think, "I can not do this?" What was it?
2. What did you do?
3. Will sharing your story help someone? Will it help your healing?

2

unprepared
for a murderer's
invasion

As Eric and Connie lay in their king-sized bed this evening before Christmas Eve many memories were being shared. The conversation had changed from the struggles of being young newlyweds to not being able to have their own children. The conversation continued with how prayers had been answered when they were able to adopt a little boy toddler, and a beautiful baby girl. Where had the years gone was the question for each other. Both children had graduated from high school; Peter was 21 and working in Eric's insurance agency. Eric had been very successful with his own agency. His business was growing with an ever-increasing client base because Eric was trusted. The word was out that he cared about his clients. Eric brought Peter into his agency to teach him the insurance business since Peter was uncertain about any special pursuit for his life. Connie had enjoyed being home on their small ranch with the children as they grew up. But now with Sue finishing her first semester of college, Eric had asked Connie to come into the office to learn the business too. Connie agreed, thinking it would take her mind off the empty nest.

Connie looked at Eric, and she saw the tears begin to trickle down his cheeks. "What is it, Eric?" "Connie, we have been so blessed and until recently, we have had a truthful, peaceful family," said Eric. "What are you talking about, Eric?" asked Connie. "I had big hopes for both our children, but I had to confront Peter yesterday," stated Eric. "Eric, confront him about what?" quizzed Connie. "About stealing from our clients," said Eric. "Stealing?" "Yes, Connie, stealing. I caught him embezzling premiums. He has taken thousands of dollars from clients' premium payments in these last few months." "Eric, how did Peter respond?" "He

> Connie looked at Eric, and she saw the tears begin to trickle down his cheeks.

stormed out of the office, making verbal threats toward me, between profane phrases." "Eric, what did he say?" asked Connie. "He said I gave him no choice but to eliminate me," answered Eric. Connie said, "No. He surely couldn't mean it. He knows how we have loved him." "Peter isn't acting like himself, Connie. He has never been mean to Sue or said any sharp words to you or me until the last few weeks. I'm not sure what he will do. I think he may have a drug problem." "Eric, not Peter," said Connie who had now joined Eric with tears and sighs.

Eric said, "Let's pray together, Connie." After their heart-wrenching prayers, the bedroom became silent until Sue popped in. "Mom and Dad, I just wanted to thank you for everything. I wanted to tell you I love you," as she kissed them both and headed down the hallway to her bedroom. Connie said, "Eric, we are blessed. Sue is proof of that." As the clock struck 1:00 a.m. ushering in Christmas Eve morning, Connie asked, "Are you still awake, Eric?" Eric wearily responded, "Yes, but not for long.

Connie, do you think Peter will come home." "I'm sure he will," said Connie. As the clock struck two, both Eric and Connie were trying to stay awake. With the sound of Peter's car pulling up, Eric says, "Finally" and closes his eyes. Connie listens as Peter enters the house. He is coming to our room, thinks Connie, maybe he is going to talk to us. Moments later Peter enters their bedroom. Eric starts to get up. A shot rings out and Eric falls back on the bed onto Connie. Sue shouts, "What is going on?" as she starts down the hall. Peter shoots and kills Sue. He then re-enters his parents' bedroom. Connie sees Peter, but is unable to speak. Her arm is over her chest with her wrist resting above her heart. Peter, at point blank range, points the gun at Connie's heart and squeezes off another round. Connie sighs, closes her eyes, and doesn't move. She knows she is going to die, too. Peter leaves the bedroom and eventually the house. Connie, still alive, manages to call the police for help.

> No one is prepared to face a murderer who invades your home in the early morning hours.

No one is prepared to face a murderer who invades your home in the early morning hours. Connie was especially unprepared when the murderer was her son. Eric and Connie had no other family, except for Connie's elderly mother. They had each other and their two children, Peter and Sue. Now if Connie would live, she would basically be all alone this Christmas. Yes, Peter had killed Eric and Sue, and then he tried to kill her. There is no way anyone can prepare for this horrific tragedy, nor would Connie be able to prepare for what was ahead.

Peter thought he would have a few days before his family would be found. He determined to head for San Diego, CA, and then cross over into Mexico. What Peter didn't know was that his

mother, Connie, was still alive. The manhunt for Peter was underway. Connie miraculously survived as the bullet intended for her
heart lodged in her wrist bones. Connie was going to live! She
would survive! Her thought was "why? Connie's protected hospital stay was filled with ugly images being replayed again and
again from Christmas Eve morning.

Those horrific images would torment Connie for years to
come. Connie was unprepared for that devastating night. She
would be unprepared for the many flashback moments ahead. She
had been a lady of great faith in her Lord, but her loss obviously
was so horrific that every foundation of her faith was crumbling.
The years of never questioning what she was facing were gone.
She had heard from other believers the partial Bible verse "the
rain falls on the just and the unjust" (Mathew 5:45b). She had had
a naive understanding of the meaning. She also knew and had
often quoted "that in all things God works for the good of those
who love Him, who have been called according to His purpose."
(Romans 8:28). "Tell me, what good can come from this?" Yes,
Connie's faith was going through the shock waves of her earth-
quake. In the weeks ahead, there would be many more severe
aftershocks and tremors that would find Connie unprepared.

Peter was apprehended in San Diego. In a few days, he would
be extradited back home to the county jail where he would be held
until his trial. The whole traumatic story was making national news
for which a very, normally private Connie was unprepared. The
news reporters were relentless, especially as the trial drew near.

Once again Connie would find herself unprepared for all the
courtroom drama with the attorneys doing their work. Finally it
was finished, so Connie thought. Peter's verdict was read,
"Guilty." Connie sighed, and then began to sob, thinking it is
finally finished. She would be unprepared for what would happen

next as the judge sat the sentencing date and asked that she be escorted to his chambers. Visibly broken, Connie set across from the judge who put his arms on his desk and began to wrench his hands together. "Connie," he said. "I can either have Peter put to death or I can give him life in prison without the possibility of parole. What would you rather I do?" Connie was once again unprepared for the judge's question. How could he ask her to make this choice? The judge said, "We have a few weeks before the sentencing date, so Connie, you take some time to answer. Connie was stunned that she would have a say as to whether Peter would live or die. Once again, she was unprepared for this testing of her faith.

With all of this unfolding, Connie needed to get away. She needed support and love. She needed listening hearts and the warmth of friends who loved her. Our phone rang and as I answered, Connie's voice said, "Could I come and stay with you and Faith for a few days? I might need to talk." "Yes, of course," was our response. But we knew that we were unprepared to know what to say or to do other than give hugs, listen, pray, and be a place of refuge for Connie.

Upon her arrival my wife and I took turns just holding Connie. She couldn't stop crying and shaking. We had no words to help at the moment. After some time passed, she shared what I have written and then asked, "What do I say to the judge?" The torment of her loss had wreaked havoc on her emotions, her spirituality, her physical being (Connie had not been able to eat), and now this mental trauma over the need to decide Peter's fate was too much. "What should I do?" (I was unprepared to just give Connie a quick, Biblical answer.)

> Connie was once again unprepared for the judge's question. How could he ask her to make this choice?

As I stated earlier, Connie's foundational faith was being put through a severe test. Satan wanted to complete the devourment of this family. "Your enemy, the devil, prowls around like a roaring lion looking for someone to devour." (1 Peter 5:8) It was becoming obvious that in our own strength we are unprepared for life's circumstances, for devastating storms, for loss, for unfamiliar transitions, and for pressure-packed choices when a time-line decision is mandated. It is an imperative faith building block to recall, "We are not fighting against flesh and blood enemies, but against evil rulers and authorities of the unseen world, against mighty powers in this dark world, and against evil spirits in the heavenly places." (Ephesians 6:12 NLT) The evil of the unseen world had entered Peter leading to the deaths of Sue and Eric and

> As more time passed, she was reminded that if you want to be forgiven you will need to give forgiveness.

the attempted murder of Connie. Now Connie, in her unpreparedness for the ongoing attack on her spiritual world, faced the personal spiritual struggle to give the judge her decision.

The Message translates 2 Corinthians 2:11 this way, "We don't want to unwittingly give Satan an opening for yet more mischief—we're not oblivious to his sly ways!" Sly indeed. Sue and Eric had been taken from Connie. Peter was just a decision away from physical death or life without parole in a federal prison. Connie knew Sue and Eric were with Jesus in heaven. But her soul, as well as Peter's soul, could hinge upon her decision for the judge. If Peter were put to death, he may not have an opportunity to come clean and to receive forgiveness. If Connie refused to choose, she knew she was making a choice. Most of us do not realize that truth. Connie knew she had to give an answer. Connie was being propped up in her soul to give the judge an answer. As more time passed, she was reminded that if you want to be forgiven you will need to give forgiveness. As she would cry out in prayer to the Lord, sometimes verses would flood her heart and mind like, "If you have anything against anyone, forgive him that your father in heaven may also forgive you your trespasses. But if you do not forgive, neither will your father in heaven forgive your trespasses." (Mark 11:25-26)

You see, it was not in Connie's strength that she was living to face another moment or another day. It was God's strength; carrying Connie along Faith Freeway with all of the improvised Satan-placed explosive, soul-wrecking devices. Yes, it is not only the war on terror in Iraq and Afghanistan where IED's are used. On life's super highway circumstances will want us to choose to exit onto Fantasy Freeway or Isolation Interstate. Both will lead to a place where pity and anger will control our choice regarding whether to forgive or not to forgive. We will be terrorized by past life circumstances, big or little, if we allow the devil to take us there again and again. Bitterness and hatred will try to remove any soul-searching to even consider forgiveness. If we choose this road, Satan wins.

Connie's day in court with the judge spoke to all who knew Connie and anything about her faith. It also spoke to the judge, and eventually it would cause Peter to spend energy being reflective regarding his mother's decision. Peter was face to face with real faith as the judge told him because of his mother he would get life in prison rather than be put to death. Connie was able to state it was only because Jesus forgave that she could forgive.

You may or may not have had someone in your own family murdered or even murdered by a close family member, but you may have experienced great loss. Life's circumstances have dealt you many devastating blows. You have been unprepared like most of us would be. You have been terrorized by the memories or the lengthy, lonely isolation times. You find you have no strength to make the next decision, yet the choice is ahead. Good news . . . as you could see, Connie was unprepared, overwhelmed, crushed, yet God came close. He strengthened her crumbling foundation of faith. Little by little Connie began to live to face another moment, even a future month. She learned again "we are being renewed day by day." (2 Corinthians 4:16) Yes, even though none of us know what a day may bring, we can learn that we can face another moment "with the strength God provides." (1 Peter 4:11)

> Unconditional love is not something given lightly or to be taken for granted.

The Holy Spirit ministered to Connie and through Connie as she lived through her unpreparedness, for events that tried to destroy the two souls who remained, as well as the countless souls of those who were observing.

Author's Comment: I know Eric would have rejoiced in Connie's decision. Eric had written me a letter just a few weeks before Peter's attack. As was Eric's way he would share his thoughts tied to God's Holy Word. He was thankful to be loved by God and to be child of God. He was quoting I John 3:1-3 then Eric said, "Think of it, Bob, sons of God." He finished by saying, ". . . now I just need His strength to live out I John 4 so that I can love and forgive Peter." This letter has meant so much to me as it emphasizes unconditional love is not something given lightly or to be taken for granted. It is to be a way of life, consciously choosing to forgive so that we can have confidence regarding our own forgiveness when we are overwhelmed with our unpreparedness for life's circumstances. Eric would have been cheering Connie's choice.

chapter 2

1. Can you put yourself in Connie's shoes for a moment and list some feelings or reactions you might have had?
2. What would you have said to the judge?
3. Would you have been able to visit Peter in prison on a regular basis? Why or why not?
4. What is the most difficult choice you would have had to make had you been Connie?

3

unprepared
for this
call

My phone ringing after midnight usually meant there was an emergency. Typically I'd be trying to wake up enough to understand who was calling and what the need was. As Jim's voice penetrated my grogginess I heard, "Pastor, forgive me for calling at this late hour, but Ellen and I really need to meet and talk with you." The hour, the sobbing, and the tone of Jim's voice told me this was very serious. Besides Jim and Ellen were normally very quiet, keep to themselves types. I agreed to meet them at the church in 45 minutes, at 2 AM.

Visibly shaken Jim and Ellen stood there outside the pastoral entrance of my office. I hugged them and we entered my office. Their body language and stifled sobs were further communication of their need for help.

"Jim and Ellen, what is it?" I asked. "It is Mark," said Jim. Mark was their only child. Mark had become very unhappy and distant with Jim and Ellen. At age 19 he left home with these words, "I'm leaving. I don't want you to look for me. When I want to see you again, I'll contact you." Jim and Ellen tried to find out what was wrong. What had they done in raising an only child that made him want to leave and have no further contact with them? Their hearts had been broken for years not knowing where Mark was, or if he was okay. They were unprepared for his actions and for the years of silence. But Jim and Ellen through all their tears had held onto God, to God's Holy Word, and to the Hope that Mark would come to know Jesus Christ as his personal Savior.

Jim said, "Pastor, we finally got a phone call from Mark just moments before we called you. It wasn't what we had been praying for, and we need your input. Mark's call caught us totally unprepared for what he said to us. We had no idea that our son had chosen the gay life-style." When he said, "Mom and dad, I have three things to say to you," we weren't prepared for what we were about to be told. Mark said, "I'm gay. I'm dying of AIDS. I do not want you to come to see me." Ellen and I had no idea. Our stunned silence must have lasted too long because Mark said, "Did you hear me?" His voice was weak but he repeated, "I'm gay. I'm dying of AIDS. I do not want you to come to see me."

> Mark's call caught us totally unprepared for what he said to us.

Finally Ellen was able to speak and through her crying said, "Son, where are you? We don't even know where you are. We have tried and tried to find you. We have prayed and prayed that you would come home." Mark said, "That is what I don't want, you and your prayers, or your Jesus. Mom, just so you know where I am when they call you after I die, I'm in the Golden Gate Hospice Care Facility in San Francisco, CA. They have strict orders not to let you and dad in, so stay home."

"Pastor, what do we do?" asked Jim.

Obviously, the prodigal son had not come to his senses or resolved any issues that had caused him to leave home. As I looked at Jim and Ellen, these good, caring parents were unprepared for the hurtful words but even more so they were unprepared for the news Mark conveyed. More than anything what kept haunting their minds were the words, "I've got AIDS. I'm dying here at this AIDS hospice." They deeply loved Mark and were baffled as well as unprepared for his continual rejection of them and their unconditional love.

> James 1:5 says,
> 'if any of you lacks
> wisdom, he should
> ask God, who gives
> generously to all
> without finding
> fault, and it will be
> given to him.'

Mark asked for a second time, "Pastor, what do we do? What would you do if this were your son?" I was unprepared to give Jim and Ellen a quick, cliché Biblical answer. Finally I took both their hands and said, "I do not have a quick fix answer for you. I know James 1:5 says, 'if any of you lacks wisdom, he should ask God, who gives generously to all without finding fault, and it will be given to him.' Together, let's ask for his wisdom," and then we prayed.

When we finished, Jim and Ellen looked at me again. "You asked what I would do if Mark was my son. Jim and Ellen, I believe in unconditional love and I know you do too. So, regardless of Mark's words tonight, I would get two plane tickets and fly to San Francisco as fast as I could." Ellen grasped Jim's hands tightly and said, "Let's go." "Yes," said Jim. "You know, pastor, even if he won't see us, he will know we are there and that should speak to him that we love him." "Absolutely, Jim. I believe God is giving wisdom and even determination right now." We prayed again asking God to order the steps of Jim and Ellen to get to

Mark, to open the door so they could see him alive one more time. Then we asked that someone would present the Good News, the plan of salvation, to Mark once again while he was still conscious. Jim and Ellen caught a flight to San Francisco from Phoenix that same day. When they arrived at San Francisco and made their way to the Golden Gate AIDS Hospice, they would be unprepared again for what they faced.

Security was in place at the AIDS hospice as Jim and Ellen tried to convey clearly that they were Mark's parents and they came from Arizona to see him. The guard said, "You will have to talk to our charge nurse and then you will know if you can see your son. Please have a seat in the conference room until she can get free."

As Jim and Ellen waited for the charge nurse for what seemed like hours, Jim called and told me what was transpiring. He asked for the church to pray. As we prayed, there came a sense that unconditional love would prevail, but first Mark needed to change his attitude and let his parents in to see him.

Patty, the charge nurse, entered the conference room and introduced herself to Jim and Ellen. She repeated Mark's wishes not to see his parents. Ellen said, "Will you tell him we are here and are not planning to leave in case he would let us see him?" "Yes," replied Patty. "I want to talk to him tonight about Jesus and I will tell him then." Jim said, "We will be praying and so will our church." Patty replied, "God is able to do the miraculous. Now why don't you go to our guest room and try to get a little bit of rest." Jim and Ellen in their physical exhaustion and emotional fatigue reluctantly agreed.

That evening as things began to slow down a little Patty made her way to Mark's room. "Mark, may I come in and talk to you for a minute?" asked Patty. Mark agreed because Patty was the first person since he had been diagnosed with AIDS to hold his hand without wearing gloves, gown or a mask. He could tell she truly cared. He could tell she was different. There was a brightness or a radiance about her very presence. "Mark," said Patty, "your parents are here. They have been here for several hours. They asked to convey their love for you. They are hoping you will allow them to come in. They really want to see you again." "I told them not to come, to stay home, but I knew they would come," said Mark. Patty said, "They must love you very much." "Yeah, unconditionally," said Mark. Patty said, "Mark, are they Christians?" "Yes, I know I have failed them and caused them pain. I couldn't live up to all the rules or standards of the church. I was struggling with my desires. I believed it would be best to leave and never come back into their lives." "But deep down you must not want that or you wouldn't have called them, right?" asked Patty. The room filled with silence as Mark turned away from looking at Patty. She was right. He wanted to know the unconditional love mom and dad said they had for him was real. Now he knew it was or they wouldn't be here. Patty saw a couple of tears being wiped away. She broke the silence with "Only Jesus in a heart can make it possible to give unconditional love." Mark's tears turned to loud sobs. "Mark, do you want Christ in your heart? Do you want peace in these last few hours you have on earth? Do you want to know the reality of the Hope Jesus brings by asking for His forgiveness? You can have peace, unconditional love, and a home in Heaven. Would you let me lead you in a prayer to receive unconditional love?" Mark turned to Patty, "Can I really be forgiven? Can I truly receive Jesus and His unconditional love?" "Yes,

> He wanted to know the unconditional love mom and dad said they had for him was real.

Mark, you can," said Patty. There are many verses in the Bible that tell us that and point us to Jesus. One of the verses often quoted is John 3:16, "For God so loved the world (that is you and me) that he gave His one and only Son, that whoever believes in him shall not perish but have eternal life." He went on in verse 17 to tell us "God did not send his Son into the world to condemn the world, but to save the world through Him." As Patty led Mark to ask forgiveness and receive Christ's unconditional love the room was filled with brightness. Joy and peace flooded Mark's heart. He looked at Patty and said, "I'm ready." "Ready?" asked Patty. "Yes," said Mark. "Ready for the journey to see Jesus, ready to see my parents and tell them they do not have to worry about me anymore. Patty, please go and get my parents." "Gladly," said Patty.

Tears of joy and long embraces welcomed Jim and Ellen into Mark's room. Once again in unpreparedness choosing to live out unconditional love brought victory out of devastation and personal defeat. A few days later I did the memorial service for Mark. What Satan intended was thwarted by Jesus and unconditional love. John 16:20 tells us from Jesus' own words that "grief will turn to joy." He shared this with his disciples as He told them about His death, His going to the Father. They were not going to understand and they would grieve over Him being gone. But the good news in their unpreparedness to deal with grief was that joy would come! Yes, as is promised in Psalm 30:5b "weeping may remain for a night, but rejoicing comes in the morning." Even in all of our circumstances where we find ourselves unprepared, if we will choose to offer unconditional love and persevere, joy will come! Ellen and Jim's estranged prodigal

> Yes, as is promised in Psalm 30:5b "weeping may remain for a night, but rejoicing comes in the morning."

found unconditional love was too much for him and his issues. It even reached past the AIDS to prepare his heart for the journey home.

Author's note: God has His people everywhere. His faithful servants show up as charge nurses, teammates, public school teachers, assembly line workers, etc. God is always trying to reach hurting, lost people. Most are surprised, maybe even unprepared when He shows up!

chapter 3

1. How would you have reacted had you been Jim or Ellen and received the shocking call from your wayward child?
2. Would you have made the trip?
3. Describe how unconditional love can turn defeat and devastation around.
4. Have you ever been surprised by God's servant or servants taking stands, and making a difference at work, at school, or in a family? Explain.

4

unprepared
to care

Being unprepared to care for a family member or a friend does not mean your heart is void of love. Until you have been called upon to experience 24 hour 7 days a week care-giving for the terminally ill family member or friend, you may not understand that you are unprepared to care. Around the clock care-giving can deplete every ounce of energy you possess. Ask any tenured hospice worker if they could give of themselves 24/7 with no end in sight. You will most likely hear what I heard, "No one can do that indefinitely. That is why we work shifts and have regular days off. It is too draining upon anyone, no matter how much you love the person, and want to help him or her."

At Thanksgiving time my wife and I found ourselves facing our unpreparedness to care. Please persevere through some background data so that you will better comprehend what we faced. It may help you someday in your response to a dying family member or friend. I hope it does because this is emotionally difficult to share.

Reliving the physical pain and emotional trauma my mother-in-law faced is very difficult. But for my mother-in-law there was also a very real spiritual war going on for her soul. She had many questions regarding faith, the church and other spiritual issues. But one of the most troubling was, "Why didn't God heal her?" She had asked. She believed. She had come to a place of calm after her cancer surgeon told her that her August surgery was successful. He said, "I got all the cancer, but this type can reoccur after a period of time." In late October, mom discovered a lump. She went to the doctor, the same cancer surgeon. He now proclaimed the cancer was back and had aggressively spread through the chest cavity. This daughter of a preacher, mother of eight, strong-willed, opinionated woman was at a crossroads as she faced her mortality.

My mother-in-law was widowed in 1972. My father-in-law, at age 50, died unexpectedly of a massive heart attack. With children still at home to raise, my mother-in-law became very independent in all of her living. But there were moments, those times when she would need help. It was in those times my wife, her oldest child, would be contacted. Through the years, I had offered many times for my mother-in-law to come and live with us. On a couple of occasions, she did. I made it clear our door was always open for her.

> This daughter of a preacher, mother of eight, strong-willed, opinionated woman was at a crossroads as she faced her mortality.

With this sampling of background information, maybe you will understand that when the phone call came on that Tuesday before Thanksgiving, I was unprepared as was my wife. Our door was open. My mother-in-law was welcomed as we picked her up from Will Rogers Airport the Friday evening after Thanksgiving. With Mom's call for help, we found ourselves totally unprepared for what was ahead. Not only was mom unprepared to face the reality of her mortality, we were unprepared for all of her "whys" and "doubts" regarding God and His promises. Her faith foundation had pretty well been demolished, and her spiritual warfare was filling our home and hearts. We were unprepared for the moving emotional moments that were occurring at a frenzied pace, the frequency of which was beginning to test our faith. It was obvious to me that mom had no peace regarding death, yet she kept assuring us that she was ready to die and would go to Heaven.

God opened a door one day to address the issue of healing. So much confusion had entered her faith world (and maybe yours) regarding physical healing from TV preachers, Faith healers, and even local pastors. I explained to Mom that when we pray the prayer of faith, we are giving God permission to touch and heal us as He sees fit. That has many more ramifications than our finite minds will compute. There was a reason Jesus prayed, "Not my will but Thy will be done" as he stood in the Garden asking that the cup of what was ahead be taken away. He was not copping out. He was not covering all His bases or showing a lack of faith. He was being submissive to God the Father, who really does know best! As I explained to mom when we ask God to heal us some of the options we can identify are: the specific issue being healed, the healing of our attitude if the physical healing we asked for doesn't occur, exercising trust no matter what God's answer is, realizing His peace so that when we leave this world we transition peacefully becoming a testimony to all who witness our physical death, and the ultimate healing takes place for us in heaven where these frail bodies and feeble emotions are made perfect. "No more tears" are shed as God wipes them away. (Revelation 7:17) Mom became very quiet and very reflective for the next few days. Faith and I continued to show her physical care and unconditional love through our Lord.

As hospice was called, we found ourselves unprepared for the flurry of activity of strangers coming and going. We were also unprepared for Mom's response as the grim reality that her time to live on earth was short. She had been confused and in denial of her real condition except for dealing with the ever-increasing pain from the cancer. On January 12 once again we were unprepared as mom said she needed to talk to both of us. She asked, "Do you have a tape recorder and tape? I want to confess and I want all of my children to get a tape of what I am about to say." As I looked at my wife's astonished face, she answered her mother with, "I need to find it." After testing the tape recorder, Mom said, "Now pray that I will say what needs to be said." Over the next almost two hours we listened to Mom's confession. She stated sins she had committed that shocked us because her image was that of being very spiritual and rigid in her beliefs. It was difficult to hear some of the sins Mom had done in light of the staunch spiritual image she had portrayed. We were unprepared to hear about those sins and to reflect on the past years of deception. We understood that "all have sinned and come short of the glory of God." (Romans 3:23) We are all sinners and only through Jesus Christ (John 14:6) are sins forgiven so that peace and hope can come into a heart. Now it was crystal clear why Mom hadn't had peace when she said that she was ready to face death and Jesus. That was not true. She had not been ready. With that realization, even though as a minister I had heard many confessions, I was unprepared for Mom's. It would answer many questions my wife had had through the years, but also create many more questions that will probably go unanswered. We were unprepared for that

As hospice was called, we found ourselves unprepared for the flurry of activity of strangers coming and going.

journey which we are still experiencing today. It is only through being recipients of His forgiveness and unconditional love that we are able to forgive and give unconditional love. That is the place where real healing begins to work. It is in that choice to forgive even when unprepared that God's words live—offering help, hope, peace, and strength. In your unpreparedness the most important choice you can make is to give unconditional love. God will prop you up if you need propping. He will give the strength for your next major moment of unpreparedness. He will do whatever is necessary if you have made the choice to forgive and love like Jesus! We are still struggling with some of Mom's confession but have consciously chosen to give it to God whenever it resurfaces.

The day after Mom's confession, she came to the table on her own to eat dinner with us. This in itself was a miracle because she had been eating only very small amounts at irregular intervals. On this day after we had given thanks, mom said, "For the first time in my life, I have peace. I feel clean inside out." Once again, we were unprepared for this blessing that has become the highlight of Mom's 74 days with us.

Less than 48 hours later we were placing mom in a hospital bed in our living room. She would never get out of that bed again, and we were unprepared for that rapid, dramatic change. Within another 72 hours she would no longer be able to open her eyes or talk with us. Twenty days after Mom was confined to the hospital bed, she peacefully went home to be with Jesus. During those twenty days of caring for her, we were unprepared to face the early morning or late night hours alone to care for her. The sounds, the emotions, the physical needs truly caught us unprepared.

The last morning Mom was with us, I heard my wife praying near her head. Listening, I heard Faith say, "Mom, it is okay to go. I want you to know that I forgive you." That was around 7AM and that afternoon Mom passed away peacefully from this world. The peace we have is knowing she was ready. God knows what He is doing even when we are unprepared. He brought her to us where she could receive physical help from my wife who is an RN, as well as from our son-in-law who is a practicing M.D. in pain management here in Edmond, OK. You see, even though we were unprepared, God had a plan to reach mom if she would listen. As her caregivers 24/7, mom got physical help and spiritual help. She may have arrived from Phoenix with her ideas about what was ahead only to find herself unprepared for what she would have to face. That state of her unpreparedness collided with the painful reality of her cancer and her mortality. She was confronted with a Savior who is always prepared. We will always believe that even though we were unprepared to care, God's will was done. Remember, He doesn't condemn. He saves. Read His words in the Holy Bible in John 3:16 and 17. See how He cares!

> God knows what He is doing even when we are unprepared.

chapter 4

1. Have you ever been caught unprepared to care? Describe what happened.

2. What is the most important choice you can make when caught unprepared to care?

3. How does Jesus reveal His care to you today?

5

unprepared
for crisis from
conflict

The vast majority of us do not like conflict. Although there are a few that seemingly love it, that is, making conflict a daily lifestyle. With conflict comes confrontational moments which we find even more displeasing. Confronting someone is something most of us are unprepared to do. As a matter of behavior many will do whatever it takes to avoid confrontation. As unprepared as we are to confront, we find ourselves even more unprepared when the confrontation over a conflict turns into a crisis. In most cases the crisis could have been avoided if forgiveness and unconditional love would have been given and accepted. Without forgiveness and unconditional love the critical conflict escalates into all out war where victims are scarred or mortally wounded. In some cases the confrontation turns deadly and

> As unprepared as we are to confront, we find ourselves even more unprepared when the confrontation over a conflict turns into a crisis.

the crisis crushes all who remain for the balance of their time on earth.

Tim had no idea that confronting his son Robby would result in a crisis within the next four hours. The conflict over curfew and the use of the family car is not uncommon among fathers and their teenage sons. Tim chose the family breakfast as the time and place to confront Robby. Besides he needed Robby's 14 year old sister to hear this message. It is Dad's house, Dad's car, and Dad's rules. You abide by them and you get the privilege of their use. Do not follow the rules and the benefits are gone. There was a confrontational storm brewing in their kitchen over the curfew and the car. This confrontational conflict got underway when Tim, in a loud authoritative voice, told Robby and Tina to sit down. As Tim started to talk his voice got louder and louder. His face and neck were scarlet. Robby was unprepared for conflict resolution and for his dad's approach, besides Robby had a lot of Tim's D.N.A. The loud voices of Robby and Tim verbally attacking each other were too much for Tina. She joined in the yelling with her own screaming. She wanted her nice, honor-student, never in trouble brother to stop yelling at dad. She wanted her loving and caring dad back. She didn't understand her dad losing control of his temper. As the anger intensified in Tim's voice, Robby jumped up from the breakfast table. Glaring at his dad, he made his way to the kitchen door leading to the carport. Tim was unprepared for his normally compliant son's reaction. He sat stunned as Robby grabbed the car keys from the hook by the door. Robby exited quickly to the carport with car keys in hand. Tim, finally getting over his son's

"Let the peace of Christ rule in your hearts, since as members of one body you were called to peace. And be thankful." (Colossians 3:15)

reaction, got up from the table and ran to the door only to see
Robby speed out of the driveway. Tim got the keys to their other
car and headed out to try to find Robby, leaving Tina standing in
the kitchen crying hysterically.

Tim's mind raced quickly over what had just transpired. He
had no idea that confronting Robby would lead to this. Tim was
thinking about stopping to call the police and reporting the inci-
dent. He realized that wouldn't help. It certainly wouldn't tell
Robby that Tim loved him. With all sorts of thoughts beginning to
flood Tim's mind they were interrupted by what Tim was seeing.
Tim would never be prepared to face this sight, yet for the rest of
his life it would be a picture that would never go away.

A hundred yards ahead was Tim's car with Robby inside.
Robby had hit a large utility pole head on. The driver's front side
of the car was smashed into the trunk. Robby was gone. There
was no saving him. He could not receive Tim's forgiveness and
unconditional love. As you can imagine, this family was devastated. Tim would struggle the rest of his life with the breakfast
table confrontation that resulted in the loss of his son. He was
unprepared to deal with his emotions and the family crisis that
turned deadly. He would be unprepared to deal with his daughter
Tina, his wife, and himself. Once again Satan had clouded the
choices available: to forgive and to love unconditionally. Over the
next several months I met with Tim on a regular basis. Tim was a
broken man who was unprepared to deal with life as he now knew
it. But the Lord came close to Tim to help him realize he still had
a daughter and a wife. He gently reminded Tim that they could
and should be the ongoing recipients of unconditional love and
forgiveness. It became clear in order for Tim to forgive himself
for that morning, he also needed to forgive Robby. With God's
help Tim was able to forgive Robby, therefore allowing Tim to

give unconditional love to Tina and his wife. I'm uncertain as to whether or not Tim ever forgave himself. To let the peace of Christ rule in our hearts before we confront is critical to conflict resolution. We are told very clearly to do just that. "Let the peace of Christ rule in your hearts, since as members of one body you were called to peace. And be thankful." (Colossians 3:15) If we do that and choose to practice the word of Christ, we will confront one another with a humble spirit full of love and forgiveness.

chapter 5

1. Describe how you view conflict.
2. Does confrontation play a positive or negative role in conflict? Explain.
3. Has lack of conflict resolution affected your relationship(s)? What can be done to bring resolve or peace?

6

unprepared
for suicide in your
microcosm

Two things stand out as extremely difficult in the duties of ministry. One is helping parents and siblings during the unexpected loss of a child, sister or brother. The other is the loss of life via suicide when that person is part of your family or close circle of friends. When your microcosm is rocked by suicide, there are often unanswered questions for which you are completely unprepared. This topic is seldom discussed except in clinical circles or grief recovery groups. It was an area of ministry for which I found myself totally unprepared. After almost ten years in ministry I was called by a family to my first suicide and asked to officiate a funeral service. What do you do? Where does one begin to try to help those left behind? How do you preach this type of funeral sermon? Is this person lost for eternity? What do you say to the family and friends that have similar difficult questions?

> When your microcosm is rocked by suicide, there are often unanswered questions for which you are completely unprepared.

After 30 years of ministry I have performed six funerals for suicide victims. I prefer to call them victims because Satan stole their will to live through various methods and through a variety of associations with mean-spirited or critical people. Sometimes he did it through the loss of a loved one, or a spouse, or even divorce. On some occasions he convinced them they were no good, losers, ugly, etc. Life no longer seemed worth living. For some their addictions clouded any possibility of clear thinking or good decision-making.

In one suicide an endless large-circled hug pulsated with each family member's sobs. On another occasion I held hands for hours in front of the ashes of a burned down house. For yet another it was sitting in the hospital waiting room staring at the floor and the ceiling while wiping away tears. Then there was telling a father his 20 some-year-old son had hanged himself. Still heart wrenching was holding the wife's hand after her husband had shot himself. When despair gives into hopelessness Satan has done his job. The Author of hope, joy, and peace does not want you to buy into Satan's lies. Satan is always out to destroy life, to steal hope. He will stop at nothing to get you to believe there isn't any purpose for living. As unprepared as we are for Satan's attacks, God is prepared. He has given us truth in His Holy Word, not lies. Jesus knew how to counter Satan. Jesus did it with God's Word! "Therefore, as God's chosen people, holy and dearly loved, clothe yourself with compassion, kindness, humility, gentleness, and patience. Bear with each other and forgive whatever griev-ances you may have against one another. Forgive as the Lord forgave you. And overall these virtues put on love, which binds them all together in perfect unity. Let the peace of Christ rule in your hearts . . . let the word of Christ dwell in you richly . . ." (Colossians 3:12-16)

As I prepared my first sermon for family and friends of a suicide victim I fasted and sought the Lord for wisdom and His words. There are those who would preach this young man straight to hell and offer no comfort for the family. I understand why because the taking of one's life is not sanctioned by God. As I fasted and prayed about this and what should be said, God made it very clear to me that He alone is the Judge, not me or anyone else! He instructed me to preach His words…not for false hope nor for our judging. He took me to Proverbs 3:5. "Trust in the Lord with all your heart and lean not on your own understanding." He reminded me again He came to save us. He clearly put into my mind Jesus on the cross with the two criminals, one on either side. He brought back the conversations that took place among the two criminals and Jesus. Then He brought to mind the one criminal's request, "Jesus, remember me when you come into your kingdom." Jesus answered him, "I tell you the truth, today you will be with me in paradise." (Luke 23:39-43) What did it mean for this funeral sermon? Soon I became convinced that as unprepared as we are to deal with suicide in our microcosm, God is still God.

> Take comfort in knowing God does not want anyone to perish, and peace with God can be made in a few seconds.

He alone is Judge. The one criminal could do nothing about his impending death but he could ask Jesus to remember him. Then the thought flooded my soul, how long does it take to say, "Jesus, remember me"? It takes less than two seconds! Try it. Time it. As we lean not on our own understanding, how long did it take that same criminal to ask Jesus to remember him? That is correct, less than two seconds. Think about it. There are times when someone commits suicide, and they consciously live for a few seconds, even minutes. This is not false hope. This is reality.

Remember there is one Judge. He alone knows where a person will spend eternity, so therefore "do not lean on your own understanding." Trust God. Take comfort in knowing God does not want anyone to perish, and peace with God can be made in a few seconds. Even though suicide can be viewed as a very selfish act by those with lots of unanswered questions who are left behind, choose to trust God with your hurt and lack of resolve.

chapter 6

1. Have you ever known anyone who committed suicide? Were you a close friend or relative?
2. What thoughts did you have about it?
3. What have you observed in others who have dealt with the suicide of someone close to   them?
4. How can you intervene to help prevent someone from making this choice?

unprepared
for criticism

You didn't ask for it, but you got it anyhow, criticism. Very few people I know like being criticized. Most of us are caught unprepared for the critic's attacks. If you are making decisions that affect others here is a news flash, you will be criticized. If you live your life from an integrity base, you will be caught unprepared by the critic who will attack your motives. Malicious, slanderous criticisms were even leveled at Jesus. Here are a few: glutton (Matthew 11:19 and Luke 7:34), Samaritan (a prejudicial, racial slur) (John 8:48), a drunkard (Luke 7:34), liar/blasphemer (Mark 14:64), deceiver (John 7:12), criminal (John 18:30), and the list of criticisms leveled at Jesus goes on. Critics are everywhere. You will face them and their cutting words throughout your life. Whether in school, or at church, or at work, or on a deserved vacation, and maybe even in the family, a critic is waiting to catch you unprepared for his negative, nit-picky, judgmental comment.

The childhood saying of "sticks and stones may break my bones, but words will never hurt me" isn't true! It wasn't true in elementary school when you were called a "tattletale" or "fatty, fatty, two by four," or "teacher's pet," or "ugly stick," and it still isn't true today. Critical words hurt. Even the so-called "constructive criticisms" have to be processed, and then acted upon to be constructive! My spiritual father, Dr. M.L. Mann used to tell me, "Bob, if you are going to answer God's call to preach and to pastor, you will need rhinoceros' hide." He was so accurate with that statement. But even the large, heavy, thick-skinned rhino has places of vulnerability. No one is fully prepared for all the various attacks the critics will level during one's life. You are vulnerable and will not be exempt. Without exception at some point in your life, you will face a critical attack fully unprepared.

So what do you do? How do you act? Do you react or do you learn to respond? Whether it is how you drive, live, or work that is being criticized, you have a choice about how you handle it. Janie had been married six times, and now Doug, her 7th husband of two and a half years, had begun to give her "constructive" criticism that was all too familiar from previous husbands. It was the critical tone and hurtful words that pushed her to divorce times six. Some of these words she heard from a critical abusive father when she was a teenager. They triggered her reactions. She admitted she was a vocal, demonstrative reactor not a contemplative responder. Jesus shows us there are times when choosing not to respond is best. The Bible teaches "without wood a fire goes out; without gossip a quarrel dies down." (Proverbs 26:20) Sometimes remaining silent, although tough to do, is the best response when caught

> Without exception at some point in your life, you will face a critical attack fully unprepared.

unprepared for criticism. But this time Janie chose to respond, to bring Doug, and to begin counseling to work through their problems. They did and are still married.

When you are unprepared for the criticism that comes in the form of an unreasonable solution or suggestion from a power-hungry critic, what do you do? It is probably not the time to go silent and stay silent. Jesus faced this from one of His own, Peter, after telling his disciples he would die and be resurrected. Peter's critique and solution for Jesus came quickly. Jesus didn't go silent but addressed his vocal critic and the critic's solution. "You are a stumbling block to me; you (Peter) do not have in mind the things of God, but the things of men." (Mark 16:23) So many times our critics do not know what has gone into the decision. They are not only void of information but foolish enough to believe they know what is best and how it should be handled. Even with this rebuke Jesus probably put Himself in Peter's place for the sake of understanding, but Jesus had to assert that He, not Peter, knew best.

As much as we are unprepared for open criticism, we find ourselves even more unprepared when the criticism comes from secretive talk and subversive planning. If we look at Jesus in His closest group of twelve, there was a betrayer. "Watch your back" is excellent advice when a betrayer is in your midst. What did Jesus do? He exposed the backstabber/betrayer. "I tell you the truth; one of you will betray me." (Matthew 26:21) Then after breaking the news (addressing publicly that He knew what was going on in secret), He exposed Judas. "Then Judas, the one who betrayed him said, 'Surely not I, Rabbi?' Jesus answered, 'Yes, it is you.'" (Matthew 26:25) Brace yourself. Just because Judas left the group, it wasn't over. But Jesus shows us it is better to have the critics outside the circle and not knowledgeable from being part of the group. It is a tough lesson for all of us who are unprepared for criticism to learn, but a very valuable lesson.

> What is important is the choice you make in regard to your response. Will you seek revenge or forgiveness?

When you have been deeply hurt maybe even suffered initial loss, i.e. job, or reputation because of unfounded criticism, the pain is powerful. It takes time and conscious effort to choose to forgive and to give unconditional love. Justice seems like a forgotten term when undue criticism has destroyed a part of your world. What is important is the choice you make in regard to your response. Will you seek revenge or forgiveness? God's Word teaches us not to take revenge. It is written: "It is mine to avenge; I will repay, says the Lord." (Romans 12:19) Choose to let God have the final say. Let Him take care of repayment. Enjoying life and moving on is the best choice you can make. Remember: "Because of the Lord's great love, we are not consumed, for His compassions never fail. They are new every morning...." (Lamentations 3:22-23) With God you can move beyond the criticism and the critic that you were unprepared to hear and to face. I know. Whether as a head football coach, athletic director, assistant superintendent of a public school, or for 29 years as a minister, I have experienced being unprepared for criticism. I have also had to face the criticism of critics. The pain for everyone is real. Let me encourage you to live by choosing God's unconditional love, forgiving, and moving on to enjoy each new day. God is prepared to deal with your critic and any criticism that may have caught you unprepared.

chapter 7

1. Given the opportunity, what would you say to your number one critic?
2. Would it hurt or help them?
3. How do you handle criticism? List some steps you would take.
4. Is there truly constructive criticism? Give an example to support your response.
5. How did Jesus deal with critics? Did He have varied responses?

unprepared
for rejection

Many images race through my mind when I think about being unprepared for rejection, all of which have varying degrees of responses and results. The NCAA Finals come to mind as the shooting guard puts up a clutch 3 pointer to win the championship but from seemingly nowhere, like a bird, comes the opponent's center that savagely blocks the shot preventing the win. It is a huge, monster rejection. The crowd in unison shouts REJECTED! Wow! That word carries a lot of hurt even if it is just a basketball game. A misguided thinker because of all he had been through, Job said, "Though He slay me, I will hope in Him." (Job 13:15) Job, thinking about rejection that could lead to death, carried on a lengthy argument until he took back his words and repented. (Job 42:5-6) Job realized God does not reject real seekers. We are going to go through testing and suffering to some degree like Jesus. (see 1 Peter 4:12-13) In our unpreparedness for rejection we must be careful to not allow ourselves to be removed from the

land of the living. Rejection that leads to isolation is one of
Satan's strategies that will lead to a devastated self-worth. I have
pastored many people who had little or no self-worth because in
their unpreparedness for rejection they moved into an isolation
lifestyle. This withdrawal mode is the
result of allowing the pain of rejection to
keep us from living. Rejection causes
deep emotional pain whose scars will
never be forgotten, but they can be
healed.

> Rejection causes
> deep emotional pain
> whose scars will
> never be forgotten,
> but they can be
> healed.

Rejection will rob us of emotional
and physical energy. It even tries to
destroy us spiritually because we now have trust and vulnerability questions. Do not let rejection destroy you. Let God, who
counts you of worth, reprogram you. Listen to Jesus' words,
"Come to me, all you who are weary and burdened, and I will
give you rest. Take my yoke upon you and learn from me, for I
am gentle and humble in heart, and you will find rest for your
souls. For my yoke is easy and my burden is light." (Mathew
11:28-33) But when you are in the grip of rejection it is hard to be
prepared to come to Jesus for a teaching session about the deeper
truths connected to rejection. God wants us to know:

- God doesn't reject us
- God says you and I are of worth
- We are made in the image of God and "God saw everything
  that He made and, said it was very good…" (Genesis 1:31)
- God wants to reprogram us
- God loves us, "Consider the incredible love God has for us
  that we should be called the children of God!.." (1 John 3:1)

Do not let rejection destroy you! Let God who counts you of value reprogram your thinking. We know from Jesus that we will experience suffering. Also the apostle Paul stated it in his letter to the Philippians, "For it has been granted to you on behalf of Christ not only to believe on Him, but also to suffer for Him." (1:29) The pain of rejection is definitely one serious form of suffering. Let me tell about Jim's suffering via personal rejection.

Jim was married and had two sons and a daughter. Jim had his own business in the city. He saw a lot of customers every week. He was well liked and knew a lot of people. Jim's father had recently received Christ into his life. Jim's dad wanted all of his sons and their families to know the peace he now had in Jesus. After several prayers and invitations Jim visited church. Jim wanted what his dad now had, that peace! Jim accepted Jesus and found the peace and hope Christ brings into a life. Jim's excitement for Jesus was contagious except with his wife. She had been raised in a cult that did not believe that Jesus is God's only son, the Savior. She leveled the ultimate rejection to Jim as she walked out on him and the three children. Unless Jim rejected his new faith in Christ, their marriage was over. Jim was unprepared for her rejection. He had been rejected by some of his old friends and he was unprepared for that too, but his wife? It was that word REJECTED that kept haunting Jim. It kept getting louder, REJECTED! Jim couldn't believe it. She had left him, not because he was coming home drunk anymore, but because he was a Christian!

> Do not let rejection destroy you! Let God who counts you of value reprogram your thinking.

Jim chose Christ. He stuck with Christ. He raised his children alone. His sufferings didn't stop with his ex-wife's rejections. In a very short period of time Jim would lose his father, his oldest son, and his only daughter to death. Jim was a modern day Job in this pastor's eyes as he stayed true to Jesus. Every Sunday or Saturday night you will find Jim playing the drums, worshipping God with the praise team. Jim chose to live for Christ regardless of the rejection and the personal loses. He continues to show his trust in his Lord and Savior. He refused to go or to stay in isolation. He did not let rejection destroy him. He easily could have gone into isolation.

Rejection is like an I.E.D. (improvised explosive device) on a Baghdad street or Iraqi roadside. It can be difficult to see coming upon it until it hits. It is intended to destroy or minimally cause serious injury to those who encounter it. Rejection tries to damage or kill a person's self-worth.

Jesus was rejected by individuals, by groups, by the religious crowd, but it had to hurt maybe the worst when He was rejected in His hometown. Talk about rejection. (Mark 6:5 & 11) What was His response? It was to live, and move on!

Regardless of who it was that rejected the blind man, he chose to trust and to follow the One who healed him!

Then there was the man, blind from birth, who encountered Jesus and received his eyesight. After being interrogated by the religious officials who were out to get Jesus, he and his parents waited for more questioning. The man was unprepared for his parents' rejection (because they were worried about their own safety) during the questioning. After that shock he chose to live and made this wonderful statement, "I was blind but now I see." (John 9:25) Regardless of who it was that rejected the blind man, he chose to trust and to follow the One who healed him! He refused to cave in to his parents' rejection that spoke of being unwanted, uncared for, and unloved. It would have been easy to withdraw, go into isolation and nurture the loneliness and rejection he experienced. "Loneliness and the feeling of being uncared for and unwanted are the greatest poverty." (Mother Teresa of Calcutta) Being overcome by the unpreparedness of unexpected rejection is a real "gut-check" for anyone but especially for a believer when it comes from other church attenders. Choose to live and forgive. Move on. Jesus did. The man born blind from birth did. Jim did. You can too! God will empower you to be victorious when unexpected rejection tries to destroy you.

chapter 8

1. How would you define rejection?
2. Have you ever felt rejection? What were your feelings?
3. How do you handle rejection?
4. How did Jesus handle rejection?

unprepared for sorrow

When the tears are no longer visible, and the crying can no longer be heard, when the chest cavity hurriedly expands and contracts, when the heartbeats race and sound like a drum getting louder and louder, you are in the grasp of deep sorrow. Who would understand this kind of pressure? Is anyone prepared for this kind of experience? It is hard to comprehend that anyone could be prepared for one of life's most intense times, a time of deep sorrow. What did Jesus do when He faced this time in His life on earth?

> It is hard to comprehend that anyone could be prepared for one of life's most intense times, a time of deep sorrow.

One of the times Jesus openly showed sorrow was at the death of Lazarus and the personal interactions that led up to the statement, "Jesus wept." (John 11:35) Was Jesus prepared for Lazarus' death or the reaction of the sisters and the disciples? Let's take a deep look at the cause of the sorrow that moved Jesus to tears. This account is found in the Bible in the Gospel of John chapter 11, verses one through forty-five.

"Now a man named Lazarus was sick. He was from Bethany, the village of Mary and her sister Martha. This Mary, whose brother Lazarus now lay sick, was the same one who poured perfume on the Lord and wiped his feet with her hair. So the sisters sent word to Jesus, 'Lord, the one you love is sick.'

When he heard this, Jesus said, 'This sickness will not end in death. (Remember this statement. I'll bring you back to it shortly.) No, it is for God's glory so that God's Son may be glorified through it.' Jesus loved Martha and her sister and Lazarus. Yet when he heard Lazarus was sick, he stayed where he was two more days. Then he said to his disciples, 'Let us go back to Judea.'

'But Rabbi,' they said, 'a short while ago the Jews tried to stone you, yet you are going back there?'

Jesus answered, 'Are there not twelve hours of daylight? A man who walks by day will not stumble, for he sees by this world's light. It is when he walks by night that he stumbles for he has no light.'

After he had said this, he went on to tell them, 'Our friend Lazarus has fallen asleep; but I am going there to wake him up.'

His disciples replied, 'Lord, if he sleeps, he will get better.' Jesus had been speaking of his death, but his disciples thought that he meant natural sleep.

So then he told them plainly, 'Lazarus is dead, and for your sake I am glad I was not there, so that you may believe. But let us go to him.'

Then Thomas said to the rest of the disciples, 'Let us also go, that we may die with him.'" (John 11:1-16)

Already we have been given some of the clues that help us understand Jesus' sorrow, as stated in verse 35 that "Jesus wept," was not caused by the actual physical death of Lazarus. He said, "This sickness will not end in death." (Verse 4) He had a purpose "that God's Son would be glorified through it." (Verse 4) The disciples were going to witness a miracle, a resurrection. In the near future if they would remember this miracle, it would help them with their sorrow at Jesus' death on the cross. It would help them when our resurrected Savior encountered them whether on the road or in a locked up room.

Hard feelings and misunderstandings flowed from Mary and Martha as you read on in chapter 11 of John. This is evidenced as Martha went out to meet Jesus and Mary stayed home. Notice that hurt caused by loss manifests itself first with the blame game. Martha addresses Jesus with, "Lord, if you had been here, my brother would not have died." (Verse 21) Although upset and having placed the blame, Martha hopes for a miracle with "but I know that even now God will give you whatever you ask." (Verse 22) Jesus responds with "Your brother will rise again." (Verse 23) Martha answers with, "I know he will rise again in the resurrection on the last day." (Verse 24) In our deep sorrow, in these painful suffering times we can misunderstand what Jesus is trying to do because of clouded perception from our hurt. It can cause us to level caustic, blaming remarks, missing the faith lesson or the miracle God wants to perform.

Now hear Jesus' words as he says to Martha, to all who are hurting, "I am the Resurrection and the Life. He who believes in me will live, even though he dies; and whoever lives and believes in me will never die. Do you believe this?" (John 11:25-26)

"Yes, Lord," Martha told him, "I believe that you are the Christ, the Son of God, who is come into the world." (John 11:27) Martha tells Mary Jesus is calling. Mary gets up quickly, going to Jesus. Those Jews who were trying to comfort Mary follow her to Jesus.

"Lord, if you had been here, my brother would not have died."
(John 11:32b) Now we are going to get another clue as to why
Jesus wept.

"When Jesus saw Mary weeping, and the Jews who had come
along with her also weeping, he was deeply moved in spirit and
troubled." (John 11:33) You see, Jesus was deeply moved over
their deep sorrow, but Jesus was also deeply troubled over their
lack of faith. Remember the Son of God is on the scene and He is
able to do miracles. They had witnessed many miracles by Jesus
before this moment. So the Lord says, "Where have you laid
him?" They said to him, "Come and see, Lord." (Verse 34) Verse
35 says, "Jesus wept."

They mistake His crying (weeping) as sorrow over Lazarus'
death. But His sorrow is over their sorrowful conditions, over
their thoughts, and their words, i.e. verse 37 "Could not he who
opened the eyes of the blind man have
kept this man from dying?" Yes, it was
their condition that made Jesus weep. He
knew all along that He would raise
Lazarus. Some may call their condition
lack of faith or total unbelief. To me their
condition is one of deep sorrow where
the pain is so great that thinking, verbalizing, even believing is
impaired. You only have to read on as Jesus approaches the tomb
and says, "'Take the stone away.' Martha protests with 'but, Lord,
by this time there is a bad odor, for he has been there four days.'"
(Verse 39) Is Martha thinking about a miracle, possibly a resurrected brother? No. Sorrow has impaired her thinking, keeping
her from believing that Jesus would or could perform a miracle.
That is what deep sorrow does, especially if it is allowed to continue for a long period of time.

> Jesus was deeply
> moved over their
> deep sorrow, but
> Jesus was also
> deeply troubled over
> their lack of faith.

"Then Jesus said, 'Did I not tell you that if you believed, you would see the Glory of God?'" (Verse 40) So they remove the stone and Jesus says, "Father I thank you that you have heard me. I knew that you always hear me, but I said this for the benefit of the people standing here, (why?) that they may believe that you sent me." (Verse 41) He proceeds to call Lazarus out and tells those witnessing this miracle to "take off the grave clothes and let him go." (Verse 44)

Is that the miracle you need today? Do you need to come out of the grave of your deep sorrow; and to be loosed from painful memories so that you can be free? That does not mean you forget the loved one you may have lost. It does mean you can cherish the good memories and move on with life. It means you can be healed of your deep sorrow. It is your choice whether to believe Jesus and live or to remain a prisoner paralyzed by the sorrow that has impaired your decisions.

For the many who have been mentioned in Unprepared they experienced Mary and Martha's pain. For the countless others I have pastored who are not mentioned, they would concur with what I have just shared. Most reached the place of choosing to trust God.

I would like us to look at another time where Jesus shows us deep sorrow. In Luke chapter 22 verses 39 through 46 we see a deeply painful scene. The sorrow is very real in Jesus and in His disciples.

"Jesus went out as usual to the Mount of Olives, and his disciples followed him. On reaching the place, he said to them, 'Pray that you will not fall into temptation.' He withdrew about a stone's throw beyond them, knelt down and prayed, 'Father, if you are willing, take this cup from me; yet not my will, but yours be done.' An angel from heaven appeared to him and strengthened him. And being in anguish, he prayed more earnestly, and his sweat was like drops of blood falling to the ground.

When Jesus arose from praying and went back to the disciples, he found them asleep, (now watch this) exhausted from sorrow. 'Why are you sleeping?' he asked them. 'Get up and pray so that you will not fall into temptation.'"

> The sorrow of mankind's sinful condition, taking on the sins of the world, facing a cruel death brought our Lord and Savior to a place of great sorrow.

Even Jesus, God's Son, sent here to be the sacrificial Lamb, under the weight of what was ahead, wanted out. The sorrow of mankind's sinful condition, taking on the sins of the world, facing a cruel death brought our Lord and Savior to a place of great sorrow. He let the struggle, and the sorrow go with "not my will, but yours be done." (Verse 42) Yes, Jesus would have liked a way out. It had become too much of a load, so much so that in his crying out to God, God sent the "angel to strengthen him." (Verse 43) The deep sorrow had brought the disciples to a place of physical exhaustion, so much so that they couldn't stay awake to pray.

You see, deep sorrow, especially if it is extended over a period of time, will bring you or me to that place of exhaustion. We learn these lessons from this sorrowful time for Jesus:

- Get to a private place with God.
- Go to the Father in prayer.
- Be submissive to God's will.
- Do not give in to temptation because of your exhausted condition.

You can overcome sorrow with God. If you need an angel to strengthen you, ask God for one. There are glorious days ahead. Listen to the Apostle Paul who definitely suffered and understood deep sorrow.

"For I consider that our present sufferings are not worth comparing with the
glory that will be revealed in us."
(Romans 8:18) Sorrow, even though we
do not want it and find ourselves unprepared for its arrival, is a way to grow and

> Choose to move
> past impaired
> thinking. Put your
> pain in God's hands.
> Trust Him!

to become more like Jesus. We are in the world and as John 16:33
states we will face trouble. "I have told you these things, so that
in me you may have peace. In this world you will have trouble.
But take heart! I have overcome the world." With Jesus you can
choose to have peace over your sorrow, it is your choice. You can
overcome your deep pain with Jesus! May I encourage you to
choose to do it!

Your loss may be of a child, or a spouse, or a parent, or a church,
or a career, wherever your sorrow has come from you can receive
God's help. Choose to move past impaired thinking. Put your pain
in God's hands. Trust Him! Maybe through our sorrow God is
teaching us to forgive and to love unconditionally.

chapter 9

1. Describe a personal event that has caused you sorrow.

2. How did you react?

3. Have you experienced relief or healing? How did that happen?

4. What part does time play, if any, in recovery from deep sorrow?

5. How did Jesus respond to sorrow?

10

unprepared
for change

As I'm writing this chapter, change became the political buzz word in the USA presidential campaigns for both major parties. They were counting heavily upon the US citizens' need or desire for change. After witnessing presidential elections for years, many a campaign has talked change but was unprepared for change.

This is often true for us. We say we want to change, maybe lose weight as an example, but are unprepared to discipline ourselves to change eating and exercise behavioral patterns. Unprepared for the price that change always requires may be a better way to say this.

Look at the USA since September 11, 2001. Osama bin Laden and his terrorist crew forced change upon the United States and the whole world. It wasn't a welcomed or a warranted change from the USA's perspective. Nevertheless, this senseless act of war put in motion the open war on terror and terrorists, as well as the billions of dollars being spent in conjunction with it. Every planned change that we prepare for has a cost, as does every change that comes that we are unprepared to face. Over the years I have listened to lots of prayers for change and have prayed for change, only to watch and hear as prayers were answered for new positions, etc, but the one asking for change hadn't weighed all the costs. Often with a new position came the requirement to relocate hundreds of miles away from family and friends. It meant starting over not just for the one asking for change but for the whole family and friends.

Change is inevitable. Look at yourself after each birthday and ask yourself have I changed? Our worlds get turned upside down or inside out because of changes that we are not prepared to encounter. The world as people knew it was about to change when God sent Jesus to earth. The majority of the world didn't even know his birth occurred. But there were some who knew even though they were unprepared. To name a few: Mary, Joseph, Elizabeth, John the Baptist, Zechariah, King Herod, the Magi, the shepherds, Simeon, and Anna the prophetess. All of these were prepared for the Messiah to come, but they were unprepared for the changes and the cost it would evoke.

> Change is inevitable. Look at yourself after each birthday and ask yourself have I changed?

To state that Jesus was a change agent would be to grossly understate what his coming would mean. Countries would war against each other because of the name of Jesus Christ and still do. Families would be divided even today. Some families reunited, yes! The world's calendar would change as a testimony of his coming with the letters A.D. and B.C. placed behind years. Centuries have come and gone, yet Jesus brings change one person at a time. People are still unprepared for Jesus. People are unprepared for the changes he will bring when he returns. Ironically, they are unprepared for his answers to their prayers.

You have probably been through a change that caught you unprepared. What was your response? Have you needed help? Where did you go to get your assistance? Being unprepared for change can bring devastating, even crippling results for any of us.

There is a Light in the darkness of your unpreparedness. There is a Hope in the seemingly hopelessness of your unpreparedness. There is a peace that goes beyond all of your understanding about your unpreparedness. That light, that hope, that peace is Jesus Christ! He offers us a choice. As free moral agents, you and I can choose how we are going to view change that confronts us whether unprepared or somewhat prepared. Being able to think and to choose is how God created us. But today there are so many things, distractions, as well as people who make it their profession to keep us from thinking and choosing. Our brains become so saturated with subliminal messages and data overload that a numbness occurs making programmed anticipated reactions the norm. The numbing of the brain is like a toxic drug that intends to remove the thinking from making choices. Keep your God-given ability to think and to choose, especially when facing change. Start by choosing to trust what God's Holy Word says about the impending change. Refuse "infomercial-data" without doing your own research before you choose.

> Keep your God-given ability to think and to choose, especially when facing change.

The disciples of Jesus were unprepared for the many changes ahead. Following the master agent of change would bring to their lives unthought-of changes. Here are a few changes that they were unprepared to face, but remember, they did.

1. The very first change had to come when Jesus said to each disciple these words, "Come, follow me." In Mathew 4:19 he

is quoted as "Come, follow me, and I will make you fishers of men." Certainly they were unprepared for the changes ahead and the choices they would have to make. It was only the beginning to walk away from Zebedee's lucrative fishing business for sons, James and John. As it is with a positive choice to follow Jesus, change not only comes to the one following but to those in his immediate circle. For example, Father Zebedee was faced with his sons leaving and who was going to take over the family business? Yes, Zebedee was caught unprepared for change.

2. Think about the changes they faced when Jesus started teaching and healing. They were unprepared for the deep truths in Matthew chapters 5, 6 & 7. No one had taught some of these practical, yet deep truths.

3. Then when the miraculous healings occurred, i.e. the man with leprosy (Matthew 8:1-4) Jesus touched the leper (they were unprepared for that act but even more unprepared for the change.) and he was healed.

Do what the disciples did. Go to Jesus. Give Him your fears regarding the change you are facing that has caught you unprepared.

Many more examples of change caught the disciples unprepared, from a Passover Supper and betrayal, to His death on the cross and Resurrection, and His Ascension. Even those closest to Him were unprepared for change. He said to them, "you of little faith, why are you so afraid?" Jesus was with them in the boat and the elements changed. Fear gripped them and they woke Jesus up with "Lord, save us! We are going to drown!" (Matthew 8:23-27) Change was about to catch them unprepared again when Jesus rebuked the elements and all was calm. Hear the disciples' wows, ooh, ahhs, and then "What kind of man is this? Even the winds and waves obey him!" (Matthew 8:27)

Do you have any unexpected elements that make you fearful of the change ahead? Maybe Jesus is onboard with you, but you are facing unbelievable change and you certainly are not calm. Do what the disciples did. Go to Jesus. Give Him your fears regarding the change you are facing that has caught you unprepared. After all Jesus speaks "Fear Not" with all authority! He has no problem putting people who are unprepared for changes in perspective. What is important is to go to Him and choose to trust Him with the change whether it caught you by surprise, unprepared, or you could see it coming but were still unable to totally prepare for it.

Change when Jesus is aboard and you have determined to trust Him will turn out for good, if you truly love Jesus. "And we know that in all things God works for the good of those who love him, who have been called according to His purpose." (Romans 8:28) "…in all these things we are more than conquerors through Jesus who loved us." (Romans 8:37) That is trust, the conscious choice we can make to be loved by Jesus and emerge victorious through the changes we face!

chapter 10

1. What is the toughest change you have ever faced?
2. Do you agree or disagree that change is inevitable?
3. What does Jesus want from us when we are faced with changes?

unprepared for a response

As hard as it is to face life altering circumstances, tragedies, or changes, we may find it equally difficult when we get a response to our questions. Through the years my wife and I have faced many changes, circumstances, and tragedies that we received no clear-cut answers for so that we could cope and move forward. We would talk together about them, pray together, and earnestly seek God's response.

One such time of a major change in our life occurred when I resigned as a head high-school football coach. I had been convicted that my life priorities were not in the order I had been proclaiming:

1. God
2. Family
3. Football

Instead honest confession revealed my real priorities:

1. Football
2. Be a college football coach
3. Family and God when football pursuits allowed

After much prayer and to show my wife and God that I meant it when I asked for forgiveness, I resigned as a head football coach. I had to get my priorities right. My questions for God were, "What do you want from me? Am I to continue to teach school? Whatever it is, Lord, I'll do it." That was in early March. A few months passed and no direction. Keeping God first was a love decision and a mind decision. My learning curve was a daily trusting and growing time. On this one particular summer day the impression to pick up my mail at the high school where I had been teaching for six years was very strong. As I entered the office to get my mail, my superintendent, Mr. Gustafason, saw me and asked if I could come down to his office. He wanted to talk to me if I had the time. As I entered his office I wondered what this was all about. My mind raced to the teaching staff since the faculty had elected me the previous year to be local teachers' union president. Mr. Gustafason took me back to his inner office study and closed the door. My mind was in overdrive because he rarely closed that door. "This must be bad," I thought. He began, "Have a seat, Bob. I want to ask you if you'll be my assistant Superintendent of Schools and Athletic Director." I was caught unprepared for that offer. "You'll start August 1 if you accept," he said. Shock would be a mild term for what I was initially feeling that day. "Mr. Gustafason, I'm honored you would

> Keeping God first was a love decision and a mind decision.

think of me for this position. You know I'll need time to pray about this." I answered. "You will have until Monday morning," he said. Three days to pray and give an answer. From union president to management, that will cause some problems for my friends, especially since I had just finished serving with six other teachers from around the state in formulating and writing the collective bargaining procedures for contract disputes.

I had never thought about being an administrator. Mr. Gustafason had certainly caught me off guard. Monday came and a very strong internal urging found me accepting the position. God had answered and I was unprepared for His response. But the position was not the only response God was bringing. He was teaching me to be his witness no matter what I am doing, where I am, or who makes up my everyday circle of people. You see, Mr. G. or Gus as he allowed a few people to call him was a no-nonsense, former WWII marine drill instructor, and an agnostic. God wanted me in this position to be His witness in the duties as assistant superintendent and as a follower of Jesus Christ. Integrity was a critical key to be able to be a witness to Gus.

After a few months into my second year as Gus' assistant, he called me back to that inner office and closed the door. That always meant that what I was about to hear would be very serious. "Please, sit down Bob." Gus sat behind his desk and stared out the window. Silence became deafening and inside I was getting uncomfortable. Finally, Gus who rarely showed any emotion cleared his throat and spoke, "I have terminal cancer, at least that is what the oncologist at the University of Michigan tells me." Once again I was unprepared for this news and Gus'

> He was teaching me to be his witness no matter what I am doing, where I am, or who makes up my everyday circle of people.

response. "I'm glad I chose you to be my assistant. I know you'll do all you can to keep the school operating efficiently during the times I'll be gone to Mexico. They have a new drug there that isn't legal in the USA. (Laetrill) They say they are having some success with it. I'm going to give it a try. You'll be in charge whenever I'm not here."

Silently I was praying for Gus and asking God to help me respond to this tough ex-marine in his hour of need. "Gus, my wife and I will be praying for you and your family. I will do everything I possibly can when you are here and when you're in Mexico to help the school run efficiently. I'll try to not leave you any problems." After a pause and knowing the relationship Gus and I had developed I added, "except the big ones." For a moment his serious stare broke into his wry smile and a brief bit of laughter. Gus said, "I knew I could count on you, now get out of here and get to work."

Wow! Silently I prayed as I left Gus's office, "Help me, Lord, to know how to help Gus. He needs your peace and your strength to face this." After many trips to Mexico, it was apparent the Laetrill wasn't working. How could I be an effective verbal witness to a man who would not be pushed? This was all happening about the time of Watergate, the late 1970's. Chuck Colson had gotten saved and written a book called Born Again. Although I had read it, I wasn't prepared to encounter God or hear His next response to my "what is next if Gus dies?" God's response to me was "Stop giving me left over time." I was humbled once again to consciously keep God in first place by living each day to the full with right priorities. "Be my witness to Gus, now!" That was the most important thing for me to do. "How?" He won't listen if I initiate a verbal testimony. The thought came, just put Colson's Born Again on your desk. Gus always looks at what is on your desk whenever he is in your office. It worked. After a few times of seeing the book on my desk, he picked it up and thumbed through it. He said, "Do you believe this stuff?" "Gus, if you mean could Chuck Colson get saved, yes, I do. The Bible tells us Jesus came to seek and to save the lost, and that he doesn't want anyone to perish. You knew I was a follower of Christ when you first hired me to be the head football coach. After all, Jesus saved me." I said. Gus put the book down and walked away. That would be my first, last and only verbal witness.

A couple of weeks later Gus walked into my office again and looked at the book. "Gus, I'm done with that book if you'd like to take it and look it over." He looked at me, and said "thanks," as he took the book. I didn't know until Gus' funeral that he had committed his life to Christ. Gus' wife was a faithful attender of a Presbyterian church. At Gus' funeral, her pastor shared about how Gus came to know Jesus in the Pastor's study just a couple of weeks before he died. Once again, I was caught unprepared for God's response as He reached Gus. It was great news to know that Gus made it to Heaven.

> The Bible tells us Jesus came to seek and to save the lost, and that he doesn't want anyone to perish.

We are interesting creatures. We call upon God in prayer, maybe asking for a miracle, and God responds. Why are we surprised when He answers? Why are we unprepared for His response? Is it a faith issue? Do we not really expect Him to answer?

The disciples had the same problem of asking yet being unprepared for His response.

"The disciples came to him and asked, 'Why do you speak to the people in parables?' He replied, 'The knowledge of the secrets of the kingdom of heaven has been given to you, but not to them. Whoever has will be given more, and he will have an abundance. Whoever does not have, even what he has will be taken from him. That is why I speak to them in parables: 'Though seeing, they do not see; though hearing, they do not hear or understand." (Matthew 13:10-13)

They were on a discipleship learning curve just as I was with His response to me. You may be there too...seeking an answer from Him but unprepared for His response.

The disciples were not ready for this response and were probably wondering if they really understood. Jesus refers to the fulfillment of Isaiah's prophecy and then says, "But blessed are your eyes because they see, and your ears because they hear." (Matthew 13:16)

They were unprepared for this response even though they had been sent out two by two to the lost sheep of Israel to preach the "Kingdom of heaven is near" message. (Matthew 10:6-7) They were on a discipleship learning curve just as I was with His response to me. You may be there too...seeking an answer from Him but unprepared for His response. God is patient with us. Look closer at these first disciples. Let's put one or two of them under the microscope to hear their questions, see Jesus' responses, and watch for unpreparedness to be revealed.

First look at Thomas with me. Jesus had been crucified and now resurrected. Thomas hears the news from the other disciples, "We have seen the Lord!" (John 20:25) Now listen to Thomas' response and the response he will need to believe. "Unless I see the nail marks in his hands and put my fingers where the nails were, and put my hand in his side, I will not believe." (John 20:25) Thomas sounds like some of us who have been through a lot. It takes a convincing response before we choose to trust again, to believe without reservation. Watch what happens. Remember Thomas asked for three things:

1. To see the nail marks in his hands
2. To put his finger where the nails had been
3. To put his hand into his side where the soldier's spear had pierced Jesus

Jesus appears to Thomas about a week later. Although all the doors were locked on this house, there is Jesus standing among them. "Peace be with you," is his greeting. "Then Jesus said to Thomas, 'Put your finger here; see my hands.' (That takes care of Thomas' first two demands.) Reach out your hand and put it into my side. (Ouch...the last demand is met.) Stop doubting and believe.'" (John 20:26-27)

After Thomas got over his unpreparedness for Jesus' response, Thomas says to Jesus, "My Lord and my God!" (John 20:28)

Before we leave this topic we need to look at Peter. He is always good for a very human reaction, especially the impetuous and the unprepared. In Matthew chapter 14 the disciples have been sent by boat to the other side of the lake while Jesus dismisses the crowd. Jesus goes up on a mountain alone to pray. Evening comes. While Jesus is alone on the mountain, the disciples, still in the boat, are quite a distance from land. They are being slowed by the wind and the waves that they are bucking. Jesus, walking on the water, approaches them. They are terrified. "It's a ghost,' they said and cried out in fear. Jesus immediately said to them, 'Take courage! It is I. Don't be afraid.'"

Enter Peter's reaction. "Lord, if it's you, tell me to come to you on the water." I doubt that Peter was truly ready for the Lord's response. Here it is, "COME." Although probably caught unprepared for that,

Peter got out of the boat (give him credit for that). Not only did Peter get out of the boat, but he "walked on the water and came toward Jesus. But when he saw the wind, (effects on the water) he was afraid and beginning to sink, (get ready for another Peter request) he cried out, 'Lord, save me!' Immediately Jesus reached out his hand and caught him. 'You of little faith,' he said, 'why did you doubt?'"

> You and I may be unprepared for His response, but we need to remember He is always prepared to respond to us and He will.

That is what Jesus wants from us, faith and trust. No doubting who he is (Thomas) or what he is able to do (Peter). You and I may be unprepared for His response, but we need to remember He is always prepared to respond to us and He will.

"Cast all your cares (anxiety) on him because he cares for you." (1 Peter 5:7)

chapter 11

1. Have you ever been surprised by a response? Describe.
2. How do priorities enter into your responses to decisions you must make?
3. Has your response ever caught anyone by surprise?
4. Did God use your response as a witness? How?

the company
of the unprepared

All around us are people who have been caught unprepared. Unprepared for the tragic loss of family or friends. Unprepared for violent acts that invade their lives. Unprepared for the phone call that brings bad news and cold, cutting words. Unprepared to step up and give 24/7 care and unconditional love to a dying family member or close friend. Unprepared for the crisis that follows the conflict. Unprepared to cope with suicide in your close circle. Unprepared for criticism, rejection and deep sorrow. Unprepared for a response, a miracle or an answer.

You see, you are not alone in your unpreparedness! There are many, many more real accounts that I could share with you about people, just like you and me that found themselves unprepared. We can be planners, visionaries, workaholics, ambitious, laborers, leaders, managers, doctors, lawyers, intelligent, educated, confident, and even competent, yet be face to face with our unpreparedness.

After World War II and the Korean War, the USA was unprepared for the cold war as it was called. A whole nation of people, the United States, had fought two major enemies at the same time and emerged victorious. For as much as December 7, 1941 (the bombing of our naval ships in Pearl Harbor) caught us unprepared, so did the term "sputnik" in the late 1950's. I was in a junior high math class when the principal and the math teacher began to admonish us that if we were good at math and science our country was going to need us. The USA was unprepared for the USSR's satellite called "sputnik" to be orbiting the earth in outer space. The fear that followed that news gripped a major part of our citizens with the thought of being unprepared for a war with the USSR who was demonstrating superiority with the "sputnik." Not to be caught totally unprepared for an attack on our homeland, bomb shelters were being sold and built by the hundreds all across America. People were taught the "duck and cover" in case of a nuclear attack.

The USA has been caught unprepared at different times throughout history. Inspirational leaders and presidents have come forward to challenge us to do something about our unpreparedness. Some of their words are now legendary and ring down through the decades, i.e. "Ask not what your country can do for you, but ask what you can do for your country." (JFK) The results were a NASA program and a man on the moon, just to name a few. "I have a dream...." (MLK) resulting in improved civil rights in America. On September 11, 2001 the USA was unprepared for the war the terrorists planned as they attempted to send "hijacked" commercial jetliners into various crucial targets. Their goal: to disrupt, to strike fear, and to catapult their cause to the center of the world stage while dealing a death blow to show the USA's vulnerability. As passengers were caught unprepared, a new saying came about with a decisive act by a group of those passengers who were determined even though they had been caught unprepared to do something. Todd Beamer's "Let's roll!" will live historically representing the choice made collectively by the passengers to keep their hijacked airliner from reaching its target, the White House.

Biblically, a large number of people were caught unprepared to face loss or to act, but they made a choice even in their unpreparedness and trusted God. Let me list a few for your perusal:

Joshua, although groomed by Moses to take over, was unprepared to hear from the Lord, "get ready to cross the Jordan River into the land (the long awaited Promised Land) I am about to give to them—to the Israelites." (Joshua 1:2) He also had to hear, "Be strong and courageous, because you will lead these people to inherit the land I swore to their forefathers to give them." (Joshua 1:6) There are times in our unpreparedness that we need to be strong and courageous, to choose to trust God.

Mary, Jesus' mother, was unprepared for the angel Gabriel's appearance but even more unprepared for his message from God. "Greetings, you who are highly favored! The Lord is with you." (Luke 1:26-28) We know that this young virgin, Mary, had to have great faith in God. The Bible tells us she was deeply

> Biblically, a large number of people were caught unprepared to face loss or to act, but they made a choice even in their unpreparedness and trusted God.

troubled by Gabriel's words and questioned what they could mean. But Gabriel told her, "Do not be afraid, Mary, you have found favor with God. You will be with child and give birth to a son, and you are to give him the name Jesus. He will be great and will be called the Son of the Most High." (Luke 1:30-32) Do you think Mary was prepared for that? Can you imagine all the thoughts and questions she would have had? What about Joseph, her fiancé? What would he say? What would he do? Would he have her stoned to death for being unfaithful in their year of engagement? After Mary's "how can this be since I am a virgin?" Gabriel explains and even with all of her unpreparedness and fear, Mary chooses to trust God with "I am the Lord's servant. May it be to me as you have said." (Luke 1:34-38)

Yes, the Bible has many people who found themselves unprepared. Was Abraham prepared to leave the familiar and his family to head out on a faith journey? Yet he chose to trust God. Do you think Noah was prepared for the neighbor's critiques, and snide remarks about his shipbuilding endeavor on dry land? What about when Sarah was told of her pregnancy at her old age? Remember she dealt with her unpreparedness by laughing at the thought of being pregnant. From lions' dens to fiery furnaces, from a pit to Pharaoh's numero uno assistant, from the fishing business to the courtyards of royalty, from a leper colony to reborn, healed citizen, the list of the unprepared goes on and on. They make up a company of faithful followers of Jesus Christ. A company that grows one person at a time. They have learned to make a choice. They use their God-given free moral agency to choose. They chose to trust God. They chose to forgive. They chose to go forward. They chose to give unconditional love.

> Every day we may face changes that catch us unprepared. But God is always prepared, and He never changes. "I the Lord do not change." (Malachi 3:6a)

You may be thinking, I'm unprepared to make any choices. I can't deal with what has caught me unprepared, whether loss or change or rejection, etc. I have exciting news! God knows exactly where you are and what you are feeling. He will help you; prepare you to get to a place where you will be able to make a choice. He will not make it for you. He doesn't want robotic servants. You need to know, even in your unpreparedness, God is prepared to help you. Every day we may face changes that catch us unprepared. But God is always prepared, and He never changes. "I the Lord do not change." (Malachi 3:6a) "Jesus Christ is the same yesterday and today and forever." (Hebrews 13:8) God also makes this promise whether we are prepared or unprepared, "Never will I leave you; never will I forsake you." (Hebrews 13:5) Therefore it is with confidence in God and the lives of the company of the unprepared who made Him their choice that I can say, "The Lord is my helper; I will not be afraid. What can man do to me?" (Hebrews 13:6)

You are never alone in your unpreparedness! Ask Connie, or Eric, or your author, or any of the others whose lives have been crushed when caught unprepared, but resurrected by God once they made that choice. What do we have when we have been caught unprepared? It may take awhile to realize it, but these three remain: "faith, hope and love. But the greatest of these is love." (1 Corinthians 13:13)

May you never forget that you may be caught unprepared, like Connie in the judge's chambers when asked, "Death or life in prison? Which do you want me to give your son?" You can choose to give unconditional love, to forgive and to trust God. Let Him help even today. Welcome to the company of the unprepared! You are in good company.

chapter 12

1. Do you see yourself in the company of the unprepared? How?
2. Do you feel alone? Are you?
3. What is your biggest trust issue?
4. What steps can you take to resolve it?

13

help for
the unprepared

A bruised reed he will not break, and a smoldering wick he will not snuff out." (Isaiah 42:3a)

If you have read this far or you are jumping to this chapter to see if the book is worth purchasing and reading, there is help for the unprepared.

"This is what the God the Lord says—he who created the heavens and stretched them out, who spread out the earth and all that comes out of it, who gives breath to its people, and life to those who walk on it: 'I, the Lord, have called you in righteousness; I will take hold of your hand. I will keep you and will make you to be a covenant for the people and a light to the Gentiles, to open eyes that are blind, to free captives from prison and to release from the dungeon those who sit in darkness. I am the Lord; that is my name!'" (Isaiah 42:5-8a)

Help is available! The Lord is the help for every unprepared person. The Lord waits for you to ask and to trust him with whatever caught you unprepared. He wants to help you. He wants to free is ready to do that. He has given us his truth to remind us who He is, Sovereign Lord. The all powerful, I AM. It starts with us believing that God can and trusting that He will. Sometimes we are like the boy's father, who brought his son to the disciples to be healed, only to be disappointed at their failure. Jesus hears from the father about their failure and says, "Bring the boy to me." Jesus asks, "How long has he been like this?" The father replies, "from childhood. This evil spirit has often thrown him into the fire or water to kill him. But if you can do anything, take pity on us and help us." "If you can?" said Jesus. "Everything is possible for him who believes."

> The Lord is the help for every unprepared person. The Lord waits for you to ask and to trust him with whatever caught you unprepared.

"Immediately the boy's father exclaimed, 'I do believe; help me overcome my unbelief!'" (Mark 9:19b-24)

That may be where you are today, wanting to believe, wanting to trust Jesus for help, yet struggling because of what has happened. You are hurting so deeply from loss, rejection, or criticism, the various topics we have touched upon, or some that we haven't that caught you by surprise. You have struggled with being so unprepared for what took place as well as your present unpreparedness. Please remember what you have read, knowing even in unbelief you can choose to ask Jesus to help you to believe.

The highway from the head to the depths of the heart is often the longest journey a person will take. Although for most of us that is a 12 to 16 inch one way highway, the choice to enter it and return to wholeness is difficult. We remain prisoners in the dark dungeon of our mind or heart, not asking Jesus to free us for life. To be able to reach that place to ask and to trust, to get help means we must know what He said. We need His words, His promises to help us reach the place that we choose to trust. Let me encourage you to read and find His promises that will help you believe. Here are a few of the ones that helped me at various times when caught unprepared. In those dark, dungeon times He would give me a phrase, or a thought, or a chapter from Him to carry me through, to face another moment, another day or maybe two. Eventually, I could choose to trust what the promise was saying to me and begin to heal and to live.

> We need His words, His promises to help us reach the place that we choose to trust.

My favorite is Psalm 91. When I've been swallowed up by some tragic, threatening circumstance that found me unprepared this series of thoughts from Psalm 91 floods my mind and heart.

> "He who dwells in the shelter
> Of the Most High
> Will rest in the shadow of
> The Almighty.
> I will say of the Lord, 'He
> Is my refuge and my fortress,
> My God, in whom I trust.'" (Psalm 91:1-2)

Inevitably, He would walk me through the whole psalm, but in crucial, life or death times would add His emphasis to these His words:

> "'Because he loves me,'" says the Lord,
> 'I will rescue him;
> I will protect him, for he
> Acknowledges my name.

He will call upon me, and I
Will answer him;
I will be with him trouble,
I will deliver him and honor him.
With long life will I satisfy him,
And show him my salvation.'"
(Psalm 91:14-16)

As his word gets inside us we can overcome unbelief, and even want to get well. Another favorite that has been very helpful to me is Psalm 121.

"I lift my eyes to the hills—
Where does my help come from?
My help comes from the Lord,
The maker of heaven and earth.
He will not let your foot slip—
He who watches over you will not slumber;
Indeed, he who watches over Israel
Will neither slumber nor sleep.
The Lord watches over you—
The Lord is your shade at your right hand;
The sun will not harm you by day,
Nor the moon by night.
The Lord will keep you from all harm—
He will watch over your life;
The Lord will watch over your coming and your going
Both now and forevermore."
(Psalm 121:1-8)

It is your choice whether you ask God for help. It is your choice whether you begin to trust God and His promises. If you do, and my sole purpose for writing Unprepared, was to encourage you to

God is prepared to help you with your unpreparedness.

make that choice, you will receive help. You see God is prepared to help you with your unpreparedness.

chapter 13

1. What does "a bruised reed he will not break, and a smoldering wick he will not snuff out" mean to you?

2. Is the "I AM" a conscious source of strength for you?

3. Are you facing something now that seems impossible?

4. Who can help you through prayer and companionship?

5. Do you have a Biblical promise to hold on to during this time? If not, ask God to give you one.

reflections

Choice is an amazing gift from God. Through my forty four years of living or trying to live the "Christ-follower" life, I am still in awe of a sovereign, holy God granting us grace and choice. In penning these final thoughts about Unprepared allow me to praise God for guiding, for reminding, and for whispering His truth again and again. Years ago He taught me He is trustworthy. He made it clear that to trust Him is a matter of individual choice. Now looking back on those early years and choices I realize how foundational they were for the tougher, more complex choices that the growing, maturing "Christ-follower" faces. His Words are true and become critical for anyone looking for answers in the face of an unexpected event or tragedy that finds us unprepared. Those faithful, trustworthy passages such as those mentioned in chapter 13 become strength for the one tangled in the debris of the unexpected life storm.

Yes, God reminded me of so many times when I was unprepared for a life event, big or small, that He was there, prepared. He taught me that if I would choose to trust Him no matter how bad it was, He had the answer, or the resource ready.

I have learned:

> At every new demand,
>> He gives needed resources.
> At every unfamiliar turn or twist in life,
>> He gives a friendly face, yes, a familiar face – His.
> Whenever I respond in obedience,
>> He responds in inspiration.
> Even before I am prepared to move in obedience,
>> He is prepared to move with His resources.

You see . . .

> Before I am hungry, the bread is prepared.
> Before I am thirsty, the water is available.
> Before I understand how, He makes a way.
> Before He calls me, He is prepared to lead me.
> Therefore, I do not need to be fearful when caught
>> unprepared.

"Nothing in all creation is hidden from God's sight. Everything is uncovered and laid bare before the eyes of Him to whom we must give account" (Hebrews 4:13, NIV). We may be unprepared, but God is prepared. Our accounting will be for our choices we make, for our obedience or disobedience.

Believing God, trusting without limits, challenges us when we have had to face being unprepared for the unexpected life tests. Over the last several months while working on Unprepared, unpreparedness has been very real to my family, to our nation, and to the world. A couple of personal examples: our second daughter and her family lost their home in North Houston on the morning of September 13, 2008 thanks to Hurricane Ike. Our youngest daughter, after several weeks of being severely sick without knowing what was wrong, experienced emergency gall bladder surgery. Our nation faced the unprecedented two plus years of political campaigning to see a first, a show down between a female candidate and an African-American to be the Democratic Party presidential nominee. History was made as the first African-American was elected to serve as President of the USA. The world, our nation, and civilization have been shocked and fearful as Wall Street plunged. Economic woes have caught people, banks, and world governments truly unprepared. Change is happening and most are unprepared for it. But reflection reminds me, God knows. God is trustworthy. God doesn't change. God is prepared, even when we are not. God reminds me that choosing to trust is our prerogative. If we would find enough faith to make the trust choice, God is prepared to act. We may be overwhelmed. We may not understand, but we can choose to trust God. We only need a mustard seed of faith.

> God is trustworthy.
> God doesn't change.
> God is prepared,
> even when we
> are not.

You see Connie, Jim, Ellen, Tim and the others whose stories you read were caught unprepared. For the majority they made a choice to trust God even though they hurt deeply and possibly didn't understand why. They lived despite the devastation and despair. They lived even though they had no strength to go on living. They lived because they chose God! You are invited to choose to trust God. An invitation always solicits a choice.

"Now to him who is able to do immeasurably more than all we ask or imagine, according to his power that is at work within us, to Him be glory . . ."
(Ephesians 3:21-21a NIV)

I have learned He is trustworthy and prepared.
My prayer would be:

"Heavenly Father,

As we traverse our daily lives amid events that catch us unprepared, may we trust You even though external mysteries would cause us to question. May our questions fade to faith despite our pain or lack of resolve. May we reflect, even through wordless prayers and feelings of being alone, upon You and Your preparedness. In our reflections may we grow to trust You more, to know You better, and to let You be Lord! In You we seek healing and peace for our souls. In You there is a resounding resolve whether we ever understand or not. You alone can confiscate our confusion from our unpreparedness and create a concrete foundation of trust for re-establishing your creation. Thank You Lord! You alone are prepared to deal with us in our state of unpreparedness. Please do. Praise Your Holy Name!"

Amen,

Dr. Robert J. Shephard

scriptures for the unprepared

In addition to the many Scriptures cited in the chapters of Unprepared, here a few more to read over and over again. If you choose to hold onto them, God will begin the healing you need. You can Trust God and His Word.

Psalm 119:89-90

[89] Your word, O LORD, is eternal;
   it stands firm in the heavens.
[90] Your faithfulness continues through all generations;
   you established the earth, and it endures.

Psalm 121:2-3

[2] My help comes from the LORD,
   the Maker of heaven and earth.
[3] He will not let your foot slip—
   he who watches over you will not slumber;

Psalm 121:8

[8] the LORD will watch over your coming and going
　　both now and forevermore.

2 Corinthians 12:9

[9] But he said to me, "My grace is sufficient for you, for my power is made perfect in weakness." Therefore I will boast all the more gladly about my weaknesses, so that Christ's power may rest on me.

Psalm 51:10-12

[10] Create in me a pure heart, O God,
　　and renew a steadfast spirit within me.
[11] Do not cast me from your presence
　　or take your Holy Spirit from me.
[12] Restore to me the joy of your salvation
　　and grant me a willing spirit, to sustain me.

Psalm 55:22

[22] Cast your cares on the LORD
　　and he will sustain you;
　　he will never let the righteous fall.

Psalm 56:4

[4] In God, whose word I praise,
　　in God I trust; I will not be afraid.
　　What can mortal man do to me?

Psalm 37:3-4

[3] Trust in the LORD and do good;
　　dwell in the land and enjoy safe pasture.
[4] Delight yourself in the LORD
　　and he will give you the desires of your heart.

Psalm 34:17-18

[17] The righteous cry out, and the LORD hears them;
   he delivers them from all their troubles.
[18] The LORD is close to the brokenhearted
   and saves those who are crushed in spirit.

Job 23:10-11

[10] But he knows the way that I take;
   when he has tested me, I will come forth as gold.
[11] My feet have closely followed his steps;
   I have kept to his way without turning aside.

Psalm 34:19

[19] A righteous man may have many troubles,
   but the LORD delivers him from them all;

Psalm 27:5

[5] For in the day of trouble
   he will keep me safe in his dwelling;
   he will hide me in the shelter of his tabernacle
   and set me high upon a rock.

Psalm 126:5

[5] Those who sow in tears
   will reap with songs of joy.

Hebrews 10:35-36

[35] So do not throw away your confidence; it will be richly rewarded.
[36] You need to persevere so that when you have done the will of God, you will receive what he has promised.

Hebrews 6:19-20

¹⁹ We have this hope as an anchor for the soul, firm and secure. It enters the inner sanctuary behind the curtain,

²⁰ where Jesus, who went before us, has entered on our behalf. He has become a high priest forever, in the order of Melchizedek.

Psalm 19:14

¹⁴ May the words of my mouth and the meditation of my heart

  be pleasing in your sight,

  O LORD, my Rock and my Redeemer.

Deuteronomy 31:6

⁶ Be strong and courageous. Do not be afraid or terrified because of them, for the LORD your God goes with you; he will never leave you nor forsake you."

Psalm 48:14

¹⁴ For this God is our God for ever and ever;

    he will be our guide even to the end.

Psalm 145:18-20

¹⁸ The LORD is near to all who call on him,

    to all who call on him in truth.

¹⁹ He fulfills the desires of those who fear him;

    he hears their cry and saves them.

²⁰ The LORD watches over all who love him,

    but all the wicked he will destroy.

Zephaniah 3:17

¹⁷ The LORD your God is with you,

    he is mighty to save.

He will take great delight in you,
he will quiet you with his love,
he will rejoice over you with singing."

Psalm 94:12-14

[12] Blessed is the man you discipline, O LORD,
the man you teach from your law;
[13] you grant him relief from days of trouble,
till a pit is dug for the wicked.
[14] For the LORD will not reject his people;
he will never forsake his inheritance.

Mark 11:24-25

[24] Therefore I tell you, whatever you ask for in prayer, believe that you have received it, and it will be yours.

[25] And when you stand praying, if you hold anything against anyone, forgive him, so that your Father in heaven may forgive you your sins."

James 4:3a

[3] When you ask, you do not receive, because you ask with wrong motives . . .

Proverbs 16:2

[2] All a man's ways seem innocent to him,
but motives are weighed by the LORD.

James 1:6-7

[6] But when he asks, he must believe and not doubt, because he who doubts is like a wave of the sea, blown and tossed by the wind.

[7] That man should not think he will receive anything from the Lord;

Matthew 9:29-30a

[29] Then he touched their eyes and said, "According to your faith will it be done to you";

[30] and their sight was restored. . .

1 John 5:14-15

[14] This is the confidence we have in approaching God: that if we ask anything according to his will, he hears us.

[15] And if we know that he hears us—whatever we ask—we know that we have what we asked of him.

Matthew 22:37-39

[37] Jesus replied: " 'Love the Lord your God with all your heart and with all your soul and with all your mind.'

[38] This is the first and greatest commandment.

[39] And the second is like it: 'Love your neighbor as yourself.

Matthew 6:33

[33] But seek first his kingdom and his righteousness, and all these things will be given to you as well.

Psalm 20:7

[7] Some trust in chariots and some in horses,
    but we trust in the name of the LORD our God.

Romans 8:38-39

[38] For I am convinced that neither death nor life, neither angels nor demons, neither the present nor the future, nor any powers,

[39] neither height nor depth, nor anything else in all creation, will be able to separate us from the love of God that is in Christ Jesus our Lord.

Ephesians 6:16

[16] In addition to all this, take up the shield of faith, with which you can extinguish all the flaming arrows of the evil one.

Philippians 1:21

[21] For to me, to live is Christ and to die is gain.

Philippians 3:20-21

[20] But our citizenship is in heaven. And we eagerly await a Savior from there, the Lord Jesus Christ,

[21] who, by the power that enables him to bring everything under his control, will transform our lowly bodies so that they will be like his glorious body.

Philippians 4:4-8

[4] Rejoice in the Lord always. I will say it again: Rejoice!

[5] Let your gentleness be evident to all. The Lord is near.

[6] Do not be anxious about anything, but in everything, by prayer and petition, with thanksgiving, present your requests to God.

[7] And the peace of God, which transcends all understanding, will guard your hearts and your minds in Christ Jesus.

[8] Finally, brothers, whatever is true, whatever is noble, whatever is right, whatever is pure, whatever is lovely, whatever is admirable—if anything is excellent or praiseworthy—think about such things.

Philippians 4:13

[13] I can do everything through him who gives me strength.

Philippians 4:19

[19] And my God will meet all your needs according to his glorious riches in Christ Jesus.

Colossians 1:13-14

[13] For he has rescued us from the dominion of darkness and brought us into the kingdom of the Son he loves,

[14] in whom we have redemption, the forgiveness of sins.

Colossians 2:2-3

[2] My purpose is that they may be encouraged in heart and united in love, so that they may have the full riches of complete understanding, in order that they may know the mystery of God, namely, Christ,

[3] in whom are hidden all the treasures of wisdom and knowledge.

Colossians 3:1-2

[1] Since, then, you have been raised with Christ, set your hearts on things above, where Christ is seated at the right hand of God.

[2] Set your minds on things above, not on earthly things.

Colossians 3:12

[12] Therefore, as God's chosen people, holy and dearly loved, clothe yourselves with compassion, kindness, humility, gentleness and patience.

Ephesians 3:20-21

[20] Now to him who is able to do immeasurably more than all we ask or imagine, according to his power that is at work within us,

[21] to him be glory in the church and in Christ Jesus throughout all generations, forever and ever! Amen.

Bible characters who were unprepared

Besides the people I mentioned in the chapter of the "Company of the Unprepared," here are a few more Biblical examples of those who were unprepared.

Consider:

- Job was unprepared for the loss of possessions and family (Job 1:13-20). He was unprepared for his three "so-called" friends' comments (Job 3-31). Job certainly didn't expect his wife to tell him, "Curse God and die" (Job 2:9).

- Jonah had been obedient to preach God's Word to people wherever God sent him. But he was unprepared when God told him to go to a people and a city he despised. Initially he could not deal with the thought of going to Ninevah, knowing that God would make salvation available to people Jonah didn't want to see saved (Jonah 1:1-3a).

- David was not prepared when Saul's favor toward him turned to jealousy and hatred, with a plot to have him killed (I Samuel 18:5-12; 19:1).
- Moses gave God his "unprepared for leadership" excuses (Exodus 3:10-13; 4:1-17).
- Hezekiah was unprepared for God's message from Isaiah regarding his impending demise (2 Kings 20:1-6).
- Jesus' disciples were unprepared for many of the lessons Jesus taught them, especially about his death and resurrection (John 16:17-22).

God offers His truth to anyone, and if chosen and followed, His Words will help bring deliverance from the shock of being caught unprepared. His Words become the prescription for hope, peace, joy, love, and healing we need when we have been victimized by the unexpected. Once again, I encourage you to choose to trust God and hold fast to His truth.

Dr. Robert J. Shephard is an ordained elder and wholly devoted servant of Jesus Christ. Bob became a follower of his Savior, Jesus Christ, in March of 1965. His spiritual journey includes eleven years in public education at the secondary level. During those years, besides college preparatory classroom teaching, Bob was a head football and head baseball coach. For three years before being called to the ministry, he served as athletic director and assistant superintendent of schools. Bob entered the ministry in June, 1979. He served four years as a denominational district administrator in Arizona. Bob has been senior pastor for five churches over a 26 year period. He earned a B.S. degree from Olivet Nazarene University, and M.A. from Western Michigan University. He also holds an honorary D.D. from Berean College. Dr. Shephard is happily married to his high school sweetheart. They have four children and 12 grandchildren.

contact information

Dr. Shephard may be contacted at 405-282-3327, or by email at bob91psalm@gmail.com. Books are available through Dr. Shephard, as well as TQL Publishing. Dr. Shephard is available for speaking.

notes

notes

notes